Collecting TODAY for TOMORROW

Collecting TODAY for TOMORROW

DAVID ALAN HERZOG

ARCO PUBLISHING, INC.
NEW YORK

Published by Arco Publishing, Inc.
219 Park Avenue South, New York, N.Y. 10003

Library of Congress Cataloging in Publication Data
Herzog, David Alan.
  Collecting today for tomorrow.

  Includes index.
  1. Radio programs—Collectibles—United
States. 2. Television programs—Collectibles—
United States. I. Title.
NK808.H44   791.44′7   79-18557

ISBN 0-668-04717-8 (Cloth Edition)
ISBN 0-668-04883-2 (Paper Edition)

Printed in the United States of America

FOR CAROL, WHO KNOWS WHY

Acknowledgments

It is never possible to put together a work such as this without owing a good deal to a great number of people. Many of the people to whom I owe a debt of gratitude I prefer not to acknowledge, for one reason or another, but then there are some very special people whose names must be mentioned.

I wish to thank Joseph W. Steele who did considerable legwork, delving, and nagging, and without whose assistance this book would have been six months overdue, which is a lot more than the three months it was actually overdue—oh, well!

A special thanks to Carol Anne Levitt Friedman, who contributed in her own unique and inimitable way to this work's being completed when it was.

My thanks to George McIntyre for the use of several photos of his most impressive premium collection.

I also must thank Lee Munsick, of the Yesteryear Shop in Boonton, New Jersey, who was more than merely helpful to a total stranger.

Penultimately, and always, my gratitude to Geoffrey Scott, Alessandra Lynn, Dylan Adrian, Jason Ari, David Todd, and Erica Suzanne.

A final thanks to my late father, George Herzog, who helped me to send away for my Lone Ranger Flashlight Ring.

Contents

Collecting TODAY for TOMORROW

Send for It Today—Yesterday

"Radio? Sure I remember it. Wasn't that television before they put the window in? But that's over and done with. Other than a little music or news, radio's heyday is over."

Sounds familiar, doesn't it? The fact of the matter, however, is that that is not at all the case. The big radio shows of the past *are* making a comeback. Oh, I don't mean that Orson Welles' *Mercury Theatre* is coming out of mothballs and will compete with prime time television, although many stations around the country are rerunning "ancient" adventure shows such as *The Shadow* and *Inner Sanctum Mysteries.* No, it's not that at all. What is happening is that millions of people are demonstrating their interest in the old shows by buying up tons of memorabilia at premium prices—premiums of the past.

The nostalgia industry is grossing uncountable millions of dollars each year, purveying the trappings of the disembodied radio voices of the past. Captain Midnight, the Lone Ranger, Hopalong Cassidy, and other characters who were superheroes a generation before the word "superhero" had even been invented are suddenly reincarnate at antique shows throughout the nation, and are cheerfully dominating mantlepieces to whose lofty heights they could not even have aspired at the zenith of their awesome power.

When the Green Hornet ruled the airwaves, his avenging buzz reverberated through the homes of thirty million Americans. One night a week, enraptured audiences hung on each eerie footfall that the sound effects technician managed to produce. Not even the most vivid imagination could conjure up the hideous danger that lurked in the shadows, waiting to spring on unsuspecting passersby.

It was not only junior and sis, either, who lay on the floor in front of the console Magnavox or leaned toward the table Philco's speaker

13

fearful of missing the least morsel of innuendo. Mom and dad were every bit as enthralled, although you might have had a tough time getting them to admit to their foible. It was, after all, I see now, no mere coincidence that whenever the family was out on Green Hornet night, we somehow always managed to get home in the nick of time. I have to confess that I never noticed the same sort of punctuality demonstrated when it was time for mother's cooking show.

On the other hand, should my Green Hornet Secret Ring have been left, accidentally to be sure, in the living room to be discovered there once the program was over, I could rely upon receiving a stern reprimand for not having taken my "junk" to my own room—where, naturally, junk belonged.

Surprise, folks! My ring is not junk any longer. In fact, it's now a priceless antique. Well ... perhaps not priceless, but it is an antique, and worth forty bucks, easily. You have to admit that that is a far cry from the 25¢ and two boxtops from god-only-knows-what that I paid for it. Today, my Green Hornet ring rates a prominent spot on the mantlepiece, right next to my Captain Marvel tie-clip and my Hoppy mug. There are, however, two difficulties with that scenario. In the first place, I don't own a mantlepiece. Had I one, in the second place I do not have any of the aforementioned trinkets to place on that mantlepiece that I don't have in the first place.

Alas, you probably don't have any of those objects either, and thereby hangs a tale. It is a tale told by an (admitted) idiot, full of no sound, a bit of fury, and signifying much. It is, in fact, the thesis of this treatise, which may perhaps best be summarized in the following manner:

If you had held onto "it," and so had everyone else, you would have been a fool, because "it" would be worthless today. Hence, you would be stuck with a space-consuming pile of junk. If, on the other hand, you had held onto "it," while everyone else had discarded theirs, today you would possess the only one of "its" kind in captivity, and could consequently name your own price, or simply give it to the Smithsonian Institution for a reasonable (read, handsome) tax deduction. Reality, of course, lies somewhere between those two extremes.

Collectibles from the not too distant past that are commanding considerable attention and concomitant prices at the time of this writing fall into, roughly, six categories:

1. Radio premiums, for which the listener sent in (by mail) a request (sometimes accompanied by a nominal fee) directly to the radio station. Tom Mix kerchiefs were usually acquired in this fashion.

2. Television premiums, which were to all intents and purposes indistinguishable from radio premiums—save, of course, for the window. The Winky Dink Magic Screen is a prime example of this ilk.

3. Comic book premiums, which proliferated for the types of characters in both of the above categories, but which were unique to many characters who were never able to make the transition to the electronic medium successfully. Red Ryder paraphernalia of all types would exemplify this particular genre.

4. Manufacturers' premiums, ranging from those offered by the various cereal companies to Ovaltine mugs, MacDonald glasses, and Coca Cola accessories of many descriptions, which represent a highly speculative area.

5. Toys and other goodies associated with some famous personality or character from radio, television or the movies, sold in stores and usually bearing the legend "official" have proven to be of lasting interest. The best investments from the motion picture category, to this date (I hasten to add), have been those things associated with cowboy stars—the "Official Hopalong Cassidy Lunch Box," to cite a more mundane f'rinstance.

6. Finally, and perhaps deservedly so from a standpoint of wide acceptance, yet definitely on the rise, is old-time commercial packaging. Just last week, I was offered a carton from the original *20 Mule Team Borax* for a mere $5.00. The carton was empty, but when it had been full, it had commanded a price of less than 20¢. Draw your own conclusion here. I should add, however, that the packaging attracting the most attention is made of metal and of glass.

It was not very long ago that antique stores and antique collectors dealt primarily in—would you believe—antiques. These were defined as furniture, jewelry, carpets, and other accessories of various description which were some hundred or more years of age. Certain other items, although younger, were considered destined to become antiques and so were sold as investments, with an eye toward their future appreciation and desirability. Tiffany lamps are an excellent example of a

In the late 1940's, Borax came out with a 20-mule-team plastic model kit.
At a recent flea market, the asking price for this particular kit was $12.

category of goods most certainly destined to become antique treasures, and even now command quite a premium despite their relative youth.

Antiques were not marked by age alone, for were that the case, any old piece of trash might have been displayable as desirable. Rather, to be counted a true specimen, an item had to exhibit excellence of craftsmanship which set it apart from the run-of-the-mill *schlock* of the day. They also represented a period of time—history, if you will—that was deemed worth remembering, or even revering. For the most part, these exemplary offerings were also hand crafted, in the tradition of the ages.

Only one of the aforementioned criteria could be considered applicable to the collectibles being examined herein. They *are* representative of a certain period of American history—a period when life was simpler, living was less expensive, and people were more naive. Many people today look back fondly, even wistfully, to that era, and so cherish the mementos that recall some of the flavor of the day.

While certainly not antiques, collectible memorabilia are showing up increasingly in the shops once exclusively devoted to the state of the art. Nostalgia is on a marked upswing as everyday life becomes more and more complicated, reaching a point where it is increasingly difficult for today's adults—the children of that earlier time—to cope with. Frequently, I am reminded of a sign which used to adorn the stucco wall of a shop in Dover, New Jersey, and which, for all I know, still does. The message on the sign read something to this effect: "We buy all kinds of junk. We sell only antiques." Try as one might, there is simply no apparent way to express it more eloquently. That sign says it all.

Still, there does appear to be a lesson here for the astute observer. A lesson besides the obvious one of "Quick, to the attic." In all candor, the attack on the attic is quite unlikely to be fruitful anyway since, judging from my own experience, you can rest assured that the Buck Rogers' ray gun was most apt to have been among your discards of four or five moves ago. No. Let us seek, rather, in the trappings of the pop culture and sub-cultures of our own time for the potential treasures of tomorrow.

Let us bear in mind that it is the trinkets of the forties and fifties that have appreciated by *one thousand* percent and more. Oh, certainly there are thirties mementos in there too, but realistically, most of the hot items don't go back more than thirty years—a far cry from that traditional hundred. Just as the children of the forties and fifties now seek to recapture the safety of the womb by surrounding themselves with the trappings of their youth, we have every reason to expect that the progeny of the sixties, seventies, and eighties will follow the same pattern.

What exorbitant sum might not a mint R2D2 command in the year 2000, when all of his (its?) identical siblings are lying upon the Tatooinian* scrap-heap? And what about a scale model of the *Enterprise*? (The one in which Leonard Nimoy spent a good part of his adult life with pointed ears, as opposed to the line of U.S. Navy vessels bearing the same designation.)

Charlie's Angels, on the other hand, are not likely to make good investments. Their following, so far, is not in the same rabid vein that makes for the creation of lasting cult figures. That is not to say, however, that I should mind a casual (or more than casual) dalliance with one of the female-oriented prototypes—don't forget Bosley. But, as a hedge against inflation, I'd opt for Snoopy or the Cookie Monster any day.

Finally, bear in mind that you, as a rational adult, are in no position

* Tatooine, I am assured by my son, Geoffrey, is Luke Skywalker's home planet in the motion-picture, *Star Wars*.

to predict what the adults of the future will covet. Nay, look to the nursery. Well, to grade school (third through eighth) anyway. Remember, it is not our grandparents, or even our parents, who are buying up Mickey Mouse autographs. If you are searching for the mysterious admirer of forties and fifties culture, you very likely need look no further than the nearest mirror. It is people in their thirties, forties, and fifties who are responsible for the nostalgia boom; those same people who were children and teenagers when the prototypes were in full flower.

Forget the A. T. & T. debentures, the Eastman Kodak preferred, and I. B. M. common stocks. Ours has been called a junk society. If, indeed, this is the case, then isn't it about time that we brought our investments into line with reality? Buy junk. Not just any junk, mind you, but select junk. The cash outlay will be minimal and, if you should guess wrong, the worst that could happen is that you would be left with a case full of trinkets for your grandchildren. If you guess correctly, however, their college tuitions would be assured. Even college costs, after all, are not rising as rapidly as Rootie Kazootie buttons.

As for the real money . . . Well, that remains for the person who can figure out how to preserve—in mint condition, mind you—a Big Mac, shake, and fries.

Now, what kind of Solar Scout would deign to part with his Buck Rogers pistol!

Chapter II

"I'm an Old Cowhand . . ."

Before supermarkets gave away trading stamps to be collected, or free gifts could be obtained by opening a new savings account, there existed a medium of exchange far more valuable to children than mere money. I refer, of course, to red and white checkerboard design box-tops from Ralston cereal. Oh, how I hated that cereal, but oh how I coveted those boxtops. Because, in those days, it never would have occurred to me to go through the cereal row at the store with my Cub Scout knife, liberating boxtops, I just gritted my teeth and swallowed my pride and my hot Ralston. Those boxtops were more important than a new radio or a lamp. They often meant life itself, for how often did Tom Mix have to summon Tony the Wonder Horse with his Whistling Siren Ring in order to be carried to safety in the nick of time? How many times did Tom need to use his real Compass Gun to vanquish the bad guys and then find his way back home? Well, if Tom needed them, how much more important was it for an ordinary Straight Shooter like me to have them?

Boxtops were the connection between the radio listener and the fantasy world that he was hearing about; the tickets that permitted physical entry to the Old West or (as we shall discuss later) the 25th Century. Boxtops bought participation in a dream that could otherwise not be entered for any amount of money.

It wasn't just Ralston boxtops of course, make no mistake about that. There were Wheaties boxtops, Ovaltine labels, even the inner seal from a jar of Cocomalt. And with the boxtop, label, or what-have-you went your pledge of eternal loyalty to your radio hero. Even more important than that, though, was that six weeks or so later—"by return mail"—came your hero's pledge of loyalty to you. Of all the sources of

19

The Tom Mix of movie fame never appeared on the radio series. Rounding up the movie bad guys kept him busy enough.

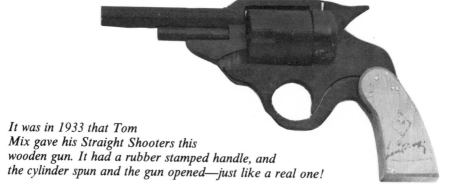

It was in 1933 that Tom Mix gave his Straight Shooters this wooden gun. It had a rubber stamped handle, and the cylinder spun and the gun opened—just like a real one!

gear from the Old West, the most bountiful treasure trove belonged to the chief Straight Shooter of them all.

Tom Mix

Tom Mix was nothing short of compulsive when it came to offering premiums. So dedicated was he, in fact, that the Tom Mix Trading Post went on offering merchandise well into 1952, even though the show had been cancelled in 1950. Apparently, the factory that had been cranking out the items had accumulated quite a stockpile, never imagining that Ralston would drop the show after eighteen years on the air. The last premiums offered were a glowing belt and the Tom Mix T-shirt, the latter featuring a picture of Curley Bradley, the radio actor who played Tom on the show. That came to pass, however, as Tony the Wonder Horse's hoofbeats were drowned out by the rocket engines of *Space Patrol* on radio *and* on television.

The first Tom Mix radio premium was, in all likelihood, the Horseshoe Nail Ring. It was a do-it-yourself type of premium, in that what you received was a horseshoe nail and instructions on how, with judicious application of pliers and poker, you might bend it to form a ring.

In common with most of the Straight Shooter manuals, the one accompanying the Horseshoe Nail Ring was primarily filled with the story of how great the real Tom Mix really was. It helped to build the legend of a soldier of fortune who rode with Teddy Roosevelt's Rough Riders, and fought in the Boxer Rebellion in China before going off to South Africa to be a hero of the Second Boer War. Then, of course, he took up the job of ridin' and ropin', being successively promoted from cowboy to Sheriff, U.S. Marshal, Texas Ranger, and movie star—with a few rodeo championships on the side, just to keep in practice. What a man!

Unfortunately, the legend of Tom Mix was just that. In point of fact, Tom Mix never left the United States during his one term in the Army, during the Spanish American War. He *was* a town marshal in Dewey, Oklahoma, for a brief stint around 1910, dealing mostly with moonshiners and bootleggers. The rest of the legend was dreamed up by the cereal company's public relations people. Nevertheless, there is something reassuring about the story in the Ralston manual—something

Tom's life story made exciting reading—bullet and knife wounds, a dynamite hole in his back. Yet they never marred his face! Golly!

The 1936 Tom Mix revolver had a cylinder which turned, but the gun no longer opened and the imprinted handles on it were made of paper.

That's Tom, on top of Tony, on top of this 1937 Silver Straight Shooter's Badge.

Tom Mix's Championship Belt Buckle (1936) is nice to own, but it's worth more with the red and white checkerboard belt attached.

Here's a pair of 1938 badges of courage. I'm sure you've noticed that Tom Mix led something of a checkered career.

Even premium sheets command a premium—$15 for this 1949 specimen. Maybe we should save A&P throwaways.

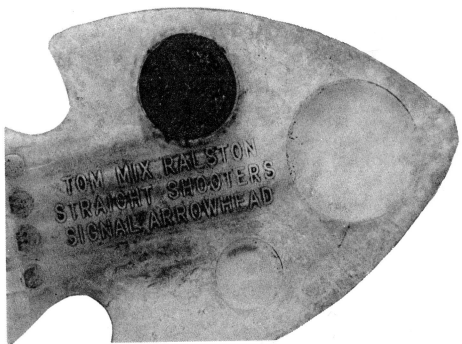

By 1949, Tom Mix's premiums were plastic—like this Signal Arrowhead. Let's get nostalgic for the Depression.

that gave every boy (and some girls) an ideal to seek to emulate. I mean, to listen to his voice on the radio (well, Curley Bradley's anyway), you knew that the chart of wounds in the manual was right. There were 12 bullet wounds, 47 bone fractures, and 22 knife wounds. The knife wounds were not shown in the chart, and neither was the 4 inch hole in his back that was caused by dynamite. Now which Tom Mix would *you* have wanted to follow on the straight and narrow path?

In 1936, Tom Mix told his loyal Straight Shooters: "I'll give you this gun. I'll send you this exact wooden model of my favorite six-shooter . . . steel black with ivory colored wood handle. The cylinder turns just like on a real revolver." It was a *real cowboy gun* for only one Ralston boxtop and 10¢ in coin to cover mailing and handling costs. "Hurry!"

Well, it really was not necessary for the radio fans to have hurried too fast, because, with various modifications, that wooden six-shooter would be available in the Tom Mix catalog of premiums until 1942. Actually, it wasn't even really brand new in 1936, having been offered as far back as 1933. Nevertheless, even in this era when metal cap pistols were universally available for less than a dollar, this wooden model attracted many kids.

Somehow, that wooden six-shooter looked more like a genuine gun than the flashy chromeplated cap pistols. It was also lightweight, easy to carry, the cylinder did spin, *and it was almost free.* The magic of Tom Mix oozed from that gun. With it in your hand, you could perform Tom's famous mirror shot. That's where Tom sights through a mirror and fires over his left shoulder to snuff out a candle being held by a bravely smiling helper twenty feet behind him. Wowee! Remember, Tom had been shot 12 times, been wounded by a knife 22 times, and injured 47 times doing movie stunts—not to mention the time he was blown up with dynamite. With this wooden gun and a little bit of luck, you might be able to lead a life just like the real Tom's! Today, depending upon its condition, that wooden gun in its cartridge belt will bring anywhere from $50 to $100.

Over the years, several different models of the "swell six-shooter" were issued. The earliest (and dearest now) was about the size of a real gun. The barrel broke open and the drum spun for a look and feel of real authenticity. That 1933 issue revolver did not even cost a dime for postage and handling. By 1939, the Tom Mix gun had become a single block of wood and had shrunken to the size of a Derringer. It also cost a dime. Any of these guns today is worth at least 500 dimes.

The original Tom Mix six-shooter was, like so many of the early radio premiums, a product of the depths of the Depression, when labor was cheap and skilled craftsmen would work their finest arts for enough money to buy a few meals. The gun's shrinkage with the passing years attested to the economy's growth. By 1940, parents had dimes to give their children, and a few dimes was all that it cost to buy a metal gun that was far more realistic in appearance than Tom's, so the six-shooter offer finally passed into oblivion.

The Lucite Signal Arrowhead, with an inscription that reads "Tom Mix Ralston Straight Shooters Signal Arrowhead," is an example of a late premium. It was offered in 1949, and was made of clear plastic. This premium was particularly distinguished by the fact that, unlike virtually all the other plastic premiums being offered at that time, it did *not* glow in the dark. The gizmo was about 4½ inches long and contained a set of four musical pipes, and a spinning siren/whistle like that used on several other Tom Mix premiums. There was also a magnifying glass and a "smallifying glass," as the reduction lens was referred to. Today, this item will fetch from $15 to $30 depending upon its condition.

Tom Mix never actually appeared on the radio series. The title role was played by a series of radio actors, including Artells Dickson, Russell Thorson, Jack Holden, and Curley Bradley. The show was created for the Ralston Company by Gardner Advertising Company—a St. Louis based firm. The multitudinous members of the Tom Mix Straight Shooters accepted a pledge that was quite similar to the Boy Scout oath, with the additional proviso that they promised to eat plenty of Ralston cereal—regularly.

So many premiums were forthcoming from Tom Mix that, beginning in 1933, Ralston began issuing a premium catalog, originally entitled *Life of Tom Mix Manual and Premium Catalog*. Today, it will cost you up to about $50 to buy one of those catalogs. A Tom Mix pocket watch that originally sold for about a dollar was created by the Ingersoll Watch Company. Exceedingly scarce today, it now sells for about $600. That is comparable to the top price at which the rarest Mickey Mouse watches have been sold of late.

TOM MIX IDENTIFICATION BRACELET

Both boys and girls will like this nifty silver flashed identification bracelet. The checkerboard design brand will remind you of the red and white box of scrumptious Hot Ralston every time you look at it. Yessirreee! It has your very own initial on it and your own number listed in Tom Mix's identification bureau. So if you ever get lost and can't remember your name, just go to the nearest policeman and ask him to find out from the Tom Mix Ralston Straight Shooters.

Bonus: With your bracelet, you will also receive a genuine fingerprint file card. Put your own fingerprints, name, and address on it and this card will be sent right to J. Edgar Hoover's F.B.I. offices in our nation's capital. It's official! Isn't that swell?

All that was yours for only 15¢ and one Ralston boxtop. Today, it would run you about $25, but the additional cost is well justified by the fact that your fingerprints, name, and address will *not* end up in the files of the F.B.I. After all, privacy is worth an additional premium.

THE SECRET DECODERS

The secret decoders were the radio craze of the thirties and forties. Orphan Annie and Captain Midnight had them too, but Tom's was the best. THE best. Needless to say, because radio premiums had to be inexpensive to manufacture they are basically, as a group, awful in design. The metal decoders, however, are the exception to the rule. They seem to defy all laws of practical economics. The sculptured metal designs exhibit the quality workmanship typical of the artisans of the thirties. The manuals that accompanied the decoders, themselves, are absolute masterpieces of graphic art, as well as being essential to using any of the devices.

The decoders appealed to the thrill of partaking in a mystery and a secret. The basic appeal of the entire craze is best described in the Tom Mix Secret Manual:

KEEP THIS BOOK IN A SECRET PLACE!

SHOW THIS BOOK ONLY TO FRIENDS WHOM YOU WANT TO BECOME STRAIGHT SHOOTERS. BUT DO NOT SHOW ANYBODY EXCEPT YOUR FAMILY THE SECTIONS MARKED *"CONFIDENTIAL!"*

As if that ominous warning were not enough, a further caveat followed:

IMPORTANT

> The information contained on these pages is very confidential. You must never reveal the SECRETS of the STRAIGHT SHOOTERS to anyone, either by telling anybody about them or by showing these pages of your Manual. *Remember to keep your Manual in a secret place!*

James Bond, eat your heart out. No secret agent had more secret stuff than a Straight Shooter. Descriptions of the Secret Salute, the Secret Password, the Secret Whistle, the Secret Grip, the Secret Flashlight Signal, and the Secret Whistle all followed the cautions. These were truly for Straight Shooters alone. One checked under the bed for spies before opening this Manual.

The super prize, though, was the Tom Mix Ralston Straight Shooters of America Official Membership Badge Decoder. Wowee! It was sculpted of high quality brass, embossed with a gorgeous Tom Mix logo and the legend "Ralston Straight Shooters of America." There were code symbols like a skull, star, key, anchor, heart, dagger, and horseshoe. A special serial number and a rotating six gun completed each simple-to-operate device. Then you just had to read the instructions.

HOW TO DECODE A SECRET MESSAGE

Each symbol on the badge stands for a secret word. HEART stands for TOMORROW; GUN means WATCH FOR; DAGGER stands for CLUE. To find the secret word, just point the gun on the badge at the symbol. The arrow on the back of the badge will then point to the secret word.

When a secret radio message is read over the air, listen for TWO things: (1.) THE NAME OF THE PERSON and (2.) A SECRET CODE SYMBOL. DISREGARD EVERYTHING ELSE! For example: Secret Message: JOHN wears an ANCHOR on his watch chain. Decoded, that means JOHN is GUILTY.

If the name of a person DOES NOT APPEAR in the secret message, then pay attention only to the CODE SYMBOL. For example: Secret Message: I saw a STAR tonight. Decoded, that means DANGER AHEAD.

REMEMBER: LISTEN ONLY FOR SECRET SYMBOLS AND NAMES OF PERSONS. PAY NO ATTENTION TO ANYTHING ELSE. With a little

*Now there's a decoder,
Straight Shooters! (1941)*

*Rings were popular even in
those days. Tom Mix was
eager to **give** away this
Spinning Siren Ring in
1944. Today, you'd be steal-
ing it at $25.*

*By 1946, Tom was con-
cerned about spies. This
Look Around Ring helped
you keep an eye on them—
and they didn't even know
you were looking.*

*Here's Tom's Magic Light
Tiger-Eye Ring (1950). Can
you imagine paying $55 for
a piece of plastic? That's
what it's going for now!
Buy two and pretend to be a
real tiger.*

*Any Tom Mix Straight
Shooter could be a real cut-up
with this 1939 pocket knife.*

practice, you can use this code in talking with other Straight Shooters, and NO ONE WILL KNOW WHAT YOU'RE SAYING!

This radio-premium offer caused a measurable increase in the sales figures for Ralston Whole Wheat Cereal and for Shredded Ralston. In addition to this marvel, millions of instant decoder buttons were produced bearing likenesses of the secondary characters on the show. There was Mike Shaw, Wash, Jane, Curley Bradley, and of course, Tony the Wonder Horse. The announcer, Don Gordon, would tell the Straight Shooters to find out whether or not Mr. Zero was the murderer by looking behind the button with the picture of Tony on it. Turning over the button, you would find the word, "GUILTY." The catch was that these buttons were packed inside boxes of Ralston Cereal, so if you wanted to know the answer, you had to get your mom to buy Ralston Cereal. (Only a very good buddy would give you the code for nothing. After all, if he had to eat Ralston to get the button, why not you?)

A Tom Mix Six Gun Decoder Badge will bring $15 to $35 today. The set of five pinback decoder buttons with instruction card is worth about $30, while individual buttons will bring $2 to $5 apiece.

RINGS ON THEIR FINGERS . . .

The premium most frequently offered by the Tom Mix show, as well as by most other radio series, was the ubiquitous ring. It had a natural appeal to kids, since their parents were seen wearing school rings, lodge rings, wedding rings, and the like. Here was an opportunity to imitate grownups, and at the same time have a mark of identification with their favorite radio hero(es).

The first Tom Mix ring offer, the Horseshoe Nail Ring, we have already discussed, but it was followed by many others. The Straight Shooters Ring of 1935 showed a raised TM Bar emblem against the checkerboard pattern of Ralston's logo. Around the edge was engraved "Tom Mix Ralston Straight Shooters." It was made of gold colored metal and adjusted to fit (or pinch) any finger. In mint condition, that ring is worth about $35 today. The year 1937 brought a signet ring which sported the wearer's initial on top with the TM Bar brand on one side, and crossed six-shooters on the other. It was offered as a good luck charm which might bring the wearer some of the same luck that had saved Tom in many dangerous encounters with grizzly bears and

Rings were made to do everything: hide messages, whistle, print initials, glow in the dark, show 8mm film, see around corners, split atoms, shoot sparks, magnify, attract metal, show compass directions, detect gold, blink light signals, and telescope. Less popular models were made simply to be worn.

mountain lions. Unfortunately, statistics are not currently available concerning the number of Straight Shooters who may have tried fighting off lions and bears with their signet rings. This ring today will bring from $25 to $50, depending upon its condition. A specimen sporting bear-claw marks on it may be worth even more.

The Mystery Ring of 1938 contained a tiny window into which one squinted to see a picture of Tom and Tony. After I spent fifteen minutes in despair trying to find that picture, and fearing that Tom was not Shooting Straight with me, my father pointed out that I had been looking in the hole that was meant to let light in. The Mystery Ring currently sells for about $25, but that price is sure to be driven down because a large quantity of them have recently been located, still in their original packing.

After the Signature Ring of 1942, and the Spinning Siren Ring of 1944, came the very popular Magnet Ring (also 1944). Priced nowadays at from $20 to $35, this ring was crowned with a small block magnet which permitted the wearer to surreptitiously pick up secret plans that were held together with steel paper clips. Believe it or not, Tom Mix actually rescued the plans for the atomic bomb from enemy agents in just that fashion.

1946 brought the Look Around Ring. Worth up to $40 today, this ring contained a tiny mirror. It was, needless to say, invaluable for looking around the corner to get advance warning of any bush-whackers that might be hiding out near the schoolhouse.

1949 brought a Sliding Whistle Ring, a device too large to actually be worn on the finger. The following year brought the last ring that old Tom ever offered. It was the Tiger Eye Ring, and it glowed in the dark. It combined lucite with a luminous plastic, so that it actually bore a re-semblance to a cat's eye. The band was a cheap golden plastic and, frankly, even though it today commands as high a price as $60 in mint condition, it still looks more like something that you would find inside a box of cereal than the sturdy sort of ring that used to demand 10¢ and a boxtop.

POSTAL TELEGRAPH SETS

In 1937, all Straight Shooters were told that "Tom's Postal Tele-graph Set is a dandy. It comes complete with International Code." Tom himself added that, "Any pal who eats Ralston can get my Signal Set *free.*"

Loads of fun in the pre-War days, the signal set was a blue card-board box with a mechanical clicker inside and the International Morse Code printed on the face. Messages would be clicked out on the radio show, which you could decipher if you had the "secret" code. The set that Tom himself carried in his pocket at all times to allow him to pick up messages out of the air was (ostensibly) a deluxe model of the very same set.

This signal set was very popular. So much so, in fact, that in 1940 an electric set was offered—complete with batteries. "Get your neighbor to send for one too. Then you can hook both sets together and send and receive messages between your house and the house next door. . . ." The set was free for two Ralston boxtops, or cost 10¢ with a single boxtop. They really and truly worked! And the set was *red.*

Since both models were made essentially of paper, they are ex-tremely rare today, and either one will bring from $23 to $50 from a serious collector.

COMPASSES TO FIND THE WAY

Perhaps Tom Mix thought that his Straight Shooters were fre-quently getting lost in the woods, or perhaps the compass was merely

Tom Mix's blue boxed Postal Telegraph Set was offered in 1937. Made of paper, it's worth up to $40 now.

The 1940 Tom Mix Compass Magnifying Glass is made of brass and worth about $40 today.

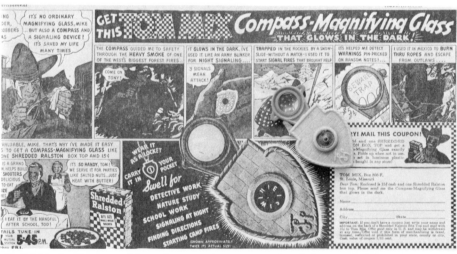

By 1946, the Compass Magnifier premium was made of glow-in-the-dark plastic. Smaller than it looked in the ad, it was still a swell thing to have if you got lost in the woods and needed to read the small type in a map to figure out which way to go.

symbolic of the aim of all Straight Shooters, which was to find the proper way through life. Whatever the reason, many compasses were offered down through the years, beginning in 1937.

The first such offer was the Compass Magnifying Glass. It was made of nickel, plated to look like silver, and was about as thick as a piece of poster-board. The compass was set into a raised oval, and the magnifying glass could be folded into or out of the oval on a single hinge. There was no identifying brand on this item, but the legend JAPAN was stamped on the back. Quite likely, it could be bought in department stores, as well as ordered from the show for a Ralston boxtop and a dime. Recently, several dealers have been asking as much as $35 for what they purport to be the original. In fact, however, it is an imitation which, in its own right, might someday be a collectible. The imitation is made of paper-thin metal and bears the legend "COMET–JAPAN" on the box inside a boxlike design. There is no box design on the thicker original.

Two or perhaps three years later, depending upon whose figures you go by, a much more attractive compass magnifier was offered by the radio show. The magnifier still folded inside the metal case that held the compass, but the case was finished in gold-colored brass and was decorated with western designs. A rope border on the front encircled a six gun, a horse's head, and a steer skull. The back sported the words "Ralston Straight Shooter" and the TM Bar brand.

Over five years passed before the Tom Mix show merchandisers decided that the world had a crying need for another compass magnifier, and by then the plastic age had arrived. The most popular plastic for radio show premiums was the kind that stored up light energy and then gave off a greenish glow in the dark—do you remember that? The Glow-in-the-Dark Compass Magnifying Glass was shaped like an arrowhead—a popular shape for many Tom Mix premiums. It bore Tom Mix's brand, the TM Bar, written in script that resembled a rope. You may find this plastic one today for as little as $12, while the earlier metal compasses can bring as much as $45.

Probably the most unusual compass ever offered by any radio show was the Gun Compass. This 1½ inch long six-shooter replica was made (for the most part) of plastic which—naturally—glowed in the dark. The barrel, however, was a metal magnet. When the gun was allowed to swing freely from the chain that it came with, the barrel would point toward the north. Attached to the non-business end of the chain was a

Butternut bread tabs of the Cisco
Kid and his sidekick, Pancho, are
available in five different colors.
Cisco is worth up to $5. That's $2
more than a Pancho tab.

Don't be surprised to see Hopalong Cassidy merchandise offered for sale at
your local flea market. There was quite a lot of it. And if you are lucky
enough to own some—hold onto it!

plastic (glowing, of course) arrowhead which also contained a whistle. Used in one fashion, the chain might form a bracelet, while in another configuration it was a keychain. Perhaps someone had seen the handwriting on the wall, because this was the first Tom Mix premium in fourteen years not to bear the TM Bar brand or some other Straight Shooter emblem upon it. Maybe the manufacturer had anticipated Tom's demise and the device's potential usefulness for another show.

The catalog of Tom Mix collectibles is enormous, as a glance at the price guide later in this book will reveal. As mentioned earlier in this chapter, the premium offers kept coming in ads and on boxes of Ralston cereals for more than a year after the show expired. This should not come as any surprise, however, if you reckon with the fact that Tom Mix himself expired ten years earlier (1940) in an automobile accident, and the show never even paused to nod toward Boot Hill. When *Tom Mix* folded, the days of the radio cowboy were over, and it was left to that upstart, television, to carry on the charisma of the Old West. Who better to take up the challenge of transition than the black clad, white mounted Hoppy.

Hopalong Cassidy

Hopalong Cassidy was a character in a book of the same name, written in 1910 by Clarence E. Mulford. The rugged but gentle leading man of a few swashbucklers, Bill Boyd, was cast in the role of "Hoppy" for the movie version of 1934. By 1946, he was able to look back upon more than sixty Hoppy flicks. Boyd, who knew a good thing when he saw it, acquired the rights to the character from Mulford in the late 1940's. When the radio series spun off from the films, naturally, he was cast in the leading role.

Hopalong Cassidy was one of several established radio series to successfully make the transition from radio to television. When the National Broadcasting Company acquired the television rights from Boyd, he naturally came along as part of the package. Boyd's hair was every bit as white as his horse Topper's before the show finally finished its television run in the 1950's.

Dozens of Hopalong Cassidy items were manufactured and marketed during the years in which the cowboy's adventures were followed by millions of fans. There were dolls, magazines, entire outfits of clothing, guns, knives, lunchpails, watches and clocks, bicycles, and even drinking glasses. Today's market for character objects is a booming one, and so it should not come as a surprise that a 20½ inch tall rubber Hoppy doll has recently commanded $75.00.

Pin-lever Hopalong Cassidy wrist watches are bringing in from $25 to $100, while comic books command $3 to $5 per copy. Hoppy jackknives currently go for about $8, and cap pistols for a minimum of $7.50. I recently saw a lunch box selling for $12, and advertising buttons going for $2 apiece. Even a drinking glass with Boyd's likeness on it has brought as much as $13, and there are plenty more Hoppy items around—their worth is just beginning to be explored. If you have any lying around, save them. They are not likely to go anywhere but up in value.

Gene Autry

Gene Autry shared with Roy Rogers the title, "King of the Cowboys." Autry, the first of the singing cowboys, came upon the scene complete with lasso, guitar, and horse in the 1930's. Autry starred in several different media, including movies, records, radio, and television. He even starred in the rodeo, in which he had considerable financial holdings. The songs that he performed in his motion pictures became best-sellers of the day on Columbia Records. The figure of Gene Autry alongside or atop Champion, the Wonder Horse, graced the front lobbies of movie theaters around the country.

After he was invited to appear on the Rudy Vallee radio show in 1936, Autry's career was well launched. The name of his home, Melody Ranch, became nearly as well known as that of the Chief Executive, President . . . er, what was his name again? Needless to say, Gene Autry dolls were marketed, as well as a number of other pieces of merchandise bearing the star's name and likeness.

Wallets and tin fan club badges, as well as books, are worth perhaps a couple of dollars apiece today. Gene Autry toy pistols, on the other hand, are worth about $60. The dolls, by the way, are worth about $25 each.

The first Gene Autry wrist watch appeared inthe 1930's, bearing the likeness on the box and watch-stand of a young, overweight cowboy whose horse is struggling to stand upright under the heavy rider. Made by the Muros Watch Company of Switzerland, that timepiece is worth about $125 today. In 1948, the watch was redesigned and issued anew by the Wilane Watch Company. It bore the likeness of an older but thinner Autry in a much more colorful design, wearing a ten gallon hat, a Pepsodent (or Doublemint) smile, and a bandolier of rifle ammunition slung over his shoulder, bandito style. The watch was "personally" inscribed on the back: "Always your pal, Gene Autry."

The Gene Autry wrist watch was such a success that it was later redesigned once more to include "action." The second hand became a six gun, and rocked back and forth to simulate the recoil of Gene's "ol' .44" that he toted when he was "back in the saddle." It was known as the Gene Autry Six-Shooter Wrist Watch and promoted as "firing 120 shots per minute."

Roy Rogers

Roy Rogers' entertainment career is something of a parallel to Gene Autry's. While Autry was just as at home in the pilot's seat of his private plane as he was in Champion's saddle, Roy, at least during his TV stint, spent more time in a Jeep than he did on Trigger's back. Roy was even more inseparable from Dale Evans, than he was from Trigger. He has also proven to be extremely durable, since he can occasionally be found, with his wife Dale, making television guest appearances on variety shows even today.

Roy Rogers starred in numerous movies, made recordings with the Sons of the Pioneers, and appeared on radio and television. He made the biggest splash of the Cassidy/Autry/Rogers trio as far as premiums were concerned. 1944 was the year in which his show first aired, sponsored by the Goodyear Tire and Rubber Company. In 1948, the Quaker Oats Company took over, and began to issue premiums. That lasted until 1953, when Post Cereals inherited the show, and the premiums started to go inside the cereal boxes. The final sponsor was the Dodge Motor Company in 1955.

Among today's prime collectible items are watches bearing the likenesses of popular stars and characters, ranging from Bill Boyd to Mickey Mouse (to Darth Vader?). Roy Rogers was no exception to this trend. Watches bring exceptionally high prices when compared to their original costs. A Roy Rogers watch made by the Ingraham Company

This Roy Rogers Sterling Silver Hat Ring has Roy's signature on the top of the brim. How about that, buckaroos?

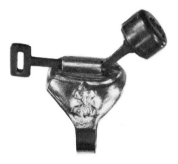

Offered in 1949, this Roy Rogers Microscope Ring can bring up to $25 today.

Remember the Roy Rogers Branding Iron Ring offered in 1948? Talk about hot stuff!

This 1950 Roy Rogers Deputy Star Badge was one of the King of the Cowboy's last radio premiums. It has a secret compartment and a whistle on the back.

will currently bring up to $80, while an Ingraham Roy Rogers alarm clock is worth from $50 to $75. The Bradley Time Corporation also made Roy Rogers watches.

Other collectibles of note which Roy's sponsors showered on his "buckaroos" were the Secret Code Manual (where have I heard that one before?) which is worth from $20 to over $30, depending upon condition, and a 1948 Branding Iron Ring (Double R Bar, of course) worth about the same. There was a Sterling Silver Hat Ring which was signed across the hat's brim. Today, that will fetch as much as $20.

Metal deputy badges run about two and a half bucks each, while a Roy Rogers camera (127 film) sells today for $6 to $10. There is a Deputy Star Badge with a secret compartment and whistle on the back that was issued in 1950. That badge will get anywhere from $10 to $18 from an avid collector. Post Metal Tab Badges, Post Pop-Out Cards, and Plastic Toby Mugs, on the other hand, are worth from $2 to $7 each. Also collectible are six inch high copper boot banks worth $13 to $17, and neckerchiefs from $8 to $15.

Gabby Hayes

Gabby Hayes was Roy Rogers' sidekick for many years. He also hosted a Quaker Cereals television show that showed serialized versions of Grade-B Western movies. He always cautioned the viewers to stand back from their television sets as he shot off the cannon containing Quaker Puffed Wheat or Quaker Puffed Rice. The Gabby Hayes

There was no chance that Gabby Hayes fans would be arrested for carrying a concealed weapon. The 1951 Shooting Cannon Ring was unconcealable.

Shooting Cannon Ring comes close to Sky King's Teleblinker as the largest ring ever produced as a premium.

The Lone Ranger

It is an old saw that the mark of the true intellectual is to be able to listen to the finale of Rossini's *William Tell Overture* without once thinking of the Lone Ranger. In all fairness, it must be observed that anyone who lives in Twentieth Century America must be culturally deprived or disoriented if he is indeed able to perform that feat. Rossini would certainly have been every bit as proud to have had his music associated with an American folk hero (fabricated though he may have been) who shot guns out of his adversaries' hands by means of silver bullets as he was of the Swiss folk hero who used a crossbow and bolt to shoot an apple off his son's head. "Return with us now to those thrilling days of yesteryear," when out of the night, the masked rider and his faithful Indian companion, Tonto, rode, with thundering hoofbeats, to warn peaceful settlers and Indians alike that a bunch of renegade whites and half-breeds were on the way.

Actors and politicians pay out hundreds of thousands of dollars to public relations agencies today to create images for them, but no image in the non-visual medium of radio was ever so powerful as that imparted to the masked man by the staff of Detroit radio station WXYZ.

It was the winter of 1932 when WXYZ station owner George W. Trendle decided to act upon his idea of creating a new western radio series. Toward that end, he got together with a young writer whom he had imported from Buffalo, New York, by the name of Fran Striker. Also present at that meeting was WXYZ's station manager, Brace Beemer. Do those names send chills up your spine? They do for' me. The basic concept for the series was Trendle's, with Striker following his lead, and Beemer contributing several details, not the least of which—later on, of course—was his voice.

The basic model for the character of the Lone Ranger was to be the masked avenger of Spanish California; a fellow called Zorro. Remember him? He was created by novelist Johnston McCulley, and was played in silent movies by Douglas Fairbanks—Senior.

The Lone Ranger first aired in 1933. In the first seven episodes, the part of the Lone Ranger was played by a man referred to as Jack Deeds. I say referred to, because after those shows nobody ever heard of him again—until a few years ago. Suddenly, a gentleman by the name of Lee Trent appeared on various interview shows claiming to be the mysterious Mr. Deeds. Regardless, the next several months saw the part taken over by George Stennius, who is now better known as motion picture director George Seaton. When he left, Brace Beemer took over. He stayed on for the better part of that first year, until he set up his own advertising agency. Earle Graser followed, and stayed with the part for several years until his accidental death in 1941, at which time Brace Beemer came back and stuck with the part until the end of the live broadcasts in 1954. *The Lone Ranger* continues in reruns today, and was, in fact, completely off the air for only five years—from 1957 through 1962.

The rapid turnover in casts during *The Lone Ranger*'s early days can be attributed to the wages paid by George W. Trendle. For working three shows a week, an actor got about $5.00. While the writers did somewhat better, they were required to make six or eight carbon copies of each show's scripts, so that Trendle could be spared the expense of having the script mimeographed. The actors who received the bottom copies had to be pretty damned good at ad libbing their parts. When, later on, the activities of actors' unions made things somewhat better, the star of the immensely popular *Lone Ranger* show was fortunate to be earning $150 per week, while small name comedians were commanding five grand.

Brace Beemer died in 1965, outlived by a horse whom he called "Silver's Pride." Beemer had appeared in many parades and rodeos before his death, riding that horse which most people took to be Silver himself.

In the early days, *The Lone Ranger* had so many local and regional sponsors that it would have been virtually impossible to keep track of all the masks, safety badges, and toy guns that were offered in different versions and at different times. The masked man helped to make a lot of dough for bread companies, and his first large regional sponsor was—coincidentally—Silvercup. The black and white photo they cautiously offered as a premium in 1935 drew such a deluge of mail that the company became instantly convinced of the character's appeal. That photo, incidentally, is today worth from $5 to $10. The same year,

Who was that masked man?

The Lone Ranger was concerned with safety in the late 1930's.

In 1943, the Lone Ranger had a pedometer. Silver had to rest sometime.

The Lone Ranger Flashlight was my favorite premium back in 1947— until I tried to find a replacement battery for it.

This 1948 Lone Ranger Six-Shooter Ring was a breeze to
operate, if you happened to have three hands.

1947 gave rise to an appropriate sou-
venir from "those thrilling days of
yesteryear"— the Lone Ranger's
Atom Bomb Ring!

The Deputy Badge that the Lone
Ranger made available to his kemo-
sabes in 1951 had a secret compartment. If you want one, it's already
worth nearly $20.

Silvercup offered a Silvercup Bread Safety Scout Membership Badge (now worth $5 to $14), and a Chief Scout Badge ($25 to $50). At the same time, Marita Bakery, which sponsored the show in the Southern region, offered a black cardboard Lone Ranger mask. It remains uncertain as to how many takers this offer received, because it is difficult to imagine how many children then were eager to wear a mask with the legend "Marita" emblazoned right between the eyes.

1938 through 1940 brought a number of Safety Club Membership Stars from those *in knead:* They came from Bond Bread, Butternut Bread, QBC Bread, and Eddy's (whatever that was). Those stars fetch between $6 and $12 today, depending upon condition.

The first airing of *The Lone Ranger* in Detroit in 1933 was not only the birth of one of the country's best and most enduring radio programs. It was also the birth of the Mutual Radio Network. In 1934, New York's radio station WOR sponsored a Lone Ranger Club. Among its earliest offered premiums were free theatre parties, admission to air meets, visits aboard American battleships, and so forth. There were even offers of free Broadway theatre tickets to the first fifty non-members who applied for club membership.

Despite the very obvious success enjoyed by the masked rider of the plains from the outset, there appeared to be some reluctance upon the part of the producers to offer premiums more closely associated with the title character. The proliferation of local sponsors has been already suggested as the probable reason, although there is also a possibility that the producers were loath to have this paragon of virtue associated with the crass considerations of pushing products. In any event, 1935 (Silvercup) brought a bit of a change, and the regional bread badges of from 1938 to 1941 marked a virtual marketing blitz. To get the campaign underway in earnest, however, remained for General Mills when it assumed national sponsorship in 1941. First Kix, and later Cheerios were promoted through *The Lone Ranger* show, and with them came a stream of premiums that lasted through the late 1950's, as the show made the successful—even spectacular—transition to television.

General Mills' takeover of coast-to-coast sponsorship meant that boxtops would bring rings and other goodies. 1941 alone brought premiums worth a total of up to $180 on today's market. They were: National Defenders Secret Portfolio, National Defenders Warning Siren, Glow-in-the-Dark Safety Belt, the 45-caliber Secret Compartment Silver Bullet (with silver ore inside), Texas Cattleman's Belt ("genuine leather" into which Lone Ranger scenes were tooled), and the Lone Ranger Polo Shirt with Hi-Yo Silver design. The Lone Ranger was off and galloping.

The year 1942 brought, among other things, the Secret Compartment Ring. This patriotic offering was available in four different versions. It came with the emblem of the Army, Navy, Air Force, or Marine Corps emblazoned on a sliding panel. Sliding back that panel revealed a tiny photograph of the Masked Man himself, plus enough room to conceal at least two microfilm copies of secret documents. Wowee, what a prize that was! (Today, it's worth from $25 to $50.) If that seems somewhat removed from the Old West ("those thrilling days of yesteryear" and all that), a 1949 offering was a ring containing 8mm movie film with scenes of the Marines landing on Iwo Jima. Then there was the Atom Bomb Ring of 1947. The front part of the bomb bears a striking resemblance to a silver bullet, but when the tail section is removed, you can see light flashes from disintegrating atoms inside.

Other rings contained flashlights, compasses, silver ore, invisible-ink pellets, and a six gun that contained a lighter-flint—so that when you fanned the flint wheel, sparks shot out, just like on a real six-shooter.

The most sought after of the Lone Ranger's offerings is a complete model of Frontier Town. Frontier Town is where the Lone Ranger and Tonto occasionally settled down for a few months of rest and relaxation after years of traveling the entire length and breadth of the West. The buildings were cut out from the backs of Cheerios boxes, but certain pieces had to be sent away for, including the gigantic map (about 12 square feet) upon which the buildings were placed. Today, the complete four sections of Frontier Town would fetch up to $200 in silver (well, certainly in coins).

Sky King

Sky King first took to the air (waves) in 1946. His real name was Schuyler, a name that made it clear that this was a person of authority and wealth. Wealth there must have been aplenty, for this flying rancher had one of the largest casts of any show in radio. There were Clipper, Penny, Jim Bell, Martha, his marvelous horse, Yellow Fury, and, naturally, the sprawling Flying Crown Ranch with a fully equipped airport to berth his *two* airplanes, Flying Arrow and the Songbird.

Sky's announcer was a person who would later go on to become something of a radio and television personality in his own right. His name was—and is—Mike Wallace.

Sky King was an apparent mixture of the most proven success aspects of *Captain Midnight* and *Tom Mix*. Together with *Jack Armstrong, All American Boy, Sky King* and its sponsors, Peter Pan Peanut Butter and Wheaties, pioneered an entirely new concept in afternoon children's adventure programming. Until *Sky King* first aired, in 1946, all such programming had been done as fifteen minute serials of the "tune in tomorrow, same time, same station" variety. Sky and Jack were half-hour complete story shows.

The two sponsors originally sought to divide the time evenly between them. So that each would pay for only seventy-five minutes per week, they hit on the plan of airing *Jack Armstrong* on Monday, Wednesday, and Friday afternoons the first week, with *Sky King* occupying Tuesday and Thursday. The following week, the order would be reversed. After an initial period of this confusing arrangement, General Mills decided to buy an additional fifteen minutes. From then on, *Jack Armstrong* went on three times a week, and *Sky King* twice.

Some of the really well written fifteen minute serials had been able to sustain interest and suspense through several episodes. The thirty minute complete stories were, however, faster moving and more enjoyable. They soon proved to be dramatic and commercial successes; so much so, in fact, that within a short time *Bobby Benson, Superman, Captain Midnight, et al.,* all jumped onto the thirty minute bandwagon. Even *Tom Mix* came into line.

The flying rancher with detective skills remained on the air until 1954, when he made the successful transition to television. Meanwhile, he celebrated his success with a modest offering of some of radio's most innovative premiums.

There were several glow-in-the-dark rings, including one that wrote secret messages with a tiny ballpoint pen, and then magnified them. Another glow-ring, the Mystery Picture Ring, showed a picture of Sky in cowpoke outfit that magically changed to a shot of him disguised as an old man. The Magni-Glo Writing Ring (1949) is worth from $15 to $30 today, while the Mystery Picture job will fetch from $25 to $40.

Sky King's Radar Signal Ring is the dearest premium from this show. It now commands as much as $70.

Wowee! A Sky King Secret Signalscope! Just what you need around the ranch, or in your private plane.

Sky King offered the largest ring ever produced for a radio show, if not the largest ring ever produced anywhere. His Tele Blinker Ring, worth from $30 to $60 today, had a luminous blinker that could be switched on and off to send messages—at night, of course. Then, the ring extended to reveal a 3½ inch telescope, so that you might see the results of your intelligence—the bad guys' hideout being blown up, for example. So large was this ring, that the Jolly Green Giant might have had trouble getting it onto his middle finger. It was not, however, the largest glow premium that old Schuyler had to offer. That meritorious claim belongs to the Secret Signalscope of 1947. The Signalscope contained a luminous signaling band, a mirror for flashing daylight messages (and looking around corners), a magnifying glass for reading enemy microfilm, and a whistle to stop escaping spies. The Signalscope's side offered code signals for warning messages such as "Look behind you," or "Danger ahead." You can buy one today for between $30 and $40.

CHAPTER III

Pre-Superheroes

The term "superhero" belongs to the 1970's, yet the character traits that distinguish a superhero from an ordinary mortal are clearly discernible in radio shows going back to the thirties. They fought for right, truth, justice, freedom, and the American way. Well, all except Sergeant Preston of the Yukon who fought for all of the preceding and the Canadian way.

Beside the venerable Mountie, there were the Green Hornet, Captain Midnight, Straight Arrow, The Shadow and others. Perhaps the most durable of them all, however, has survived the seventies in fine fettle and may go on forever—I'm not sure what the average life span is on Krypton.

Superman

The Adventures of Superman burst onto the Mutual Radio Network in 1940, after having been created by Jerome Siegel and Joe Schuster. (Siegel and Schuster's Man of Steel first saw the light of Earth in Action Comics. The year was 1938.) The radio show's opening had to be one of radio's best and most memorable, alongside the *Lone Ranger*'s:

SDFX: RIFLE SHOT AND RICOCHET
ANNOUNCER: Faster than a speeding bullet . . .
SDFX: STEAM LOCOMOTIVE AT FULL SPEED
ANNOUNCER: More powerful than a locomotive . . .
SDFX: RUSH OF WIND
ANNOUNCER: Able to leap tall buildings at a single bound . . .
MAN: Look! . . . Up in the sky! . . . It's a bird! . . . It's a plane! . . .
ANNOUNCER: It's Superman!

Music and additional background information followed.

Bud Collyer—that's right, the same Bud Collyer that most people would remember as the mild mannered TV host of the game show, *Beat the Clock*—played mild mannered reporter, Clark Kent. A simple voice change and he was Superman. The characters on the show were already familiar to the audience from the comic books, so the listener's mind made a perfect stage for some of the Man of Steel's more spectacular exploits.

Most of the surviving taped episodes of the fifteen minute serial—which went to half hour complete adventures in 1949—pitted the Kryptonian against the Nazis. Kellogg's Pep (the super delicious cereal) was responsible for a number of war planes and military buttons. They came inside the cereal boxes.

Strong and fast though Superman may have been, he was not so super when it came to giving away premiums. The best of the lot was a silver embossed ring with the hero's likeness on it. Today, the Superman Crusader's Ring will bring from $35 to $70.

Superman's Crusaders stood for religious and racial equality, and the show's story line usually drove home this message with a sledge hammer. They unearthed a plethora of philanthropic Jewish baseball stars, prizefighting Catholic priests, and blacks who were a credit to their race.

Actual character premiums were very few, but in 1942 Superman–Tim premiums began to appear. At first, they had no connection with the radio show, being a clothing store promotion to building up the clientele. Later, however, when the show took local spot announcements, many stores tied the promotion together with the show. These Superman–Tim premiums include Membership Buttons ($10 to $25), Tim Club Ring ($20 to $50), and Superman Good Stuff Sweatshirt ($18 to $35).

First appearing in 1944, in denominations of 1, 5, 10, and 20, were Superman Red Backs. These "bills" could be redeemed for toys and other prizes. While the toys and such were not premiums, the Red Backs themselves are worth from 2 to 6 greenbacks nowadays.

The radio series became so popular that youngsters thronged to join the Superman Club of America. They wore pins to aver their faithfulness. The pins, which were offered originally as radio premiums, are worth about $20 each today, despite the fact that they are made of celluloid.

Superman's Crusaders Ring was offered in the early 1940's. If you wanted to buy one now, you'd have to go a lot higher than the early 40's.

Kellogg's Pep offered this Silver Metal Airplane Ring on the **Superman** *show in 1948.*

This stud pin was a pulp premium for The Shadow. In mint condition, it will bring about $120.

The celebrated Blue Coal Glow-in-the-Dark Ring offered by The Shadow can bring $170. And it's plastic!

The Shadow also put out this Crocodile Ring in 1947. Made of plastic with a black stone, it was offered by Carey Salt. At $75, it's now worth many times its weight in the sponsor's product.

The radio show aired for the last time in 1951 . . . but Superman, the Man of Steel, goes on.

The Shadow

"Who knows what evil lurks in the hearts of men?" Well, by now it is to be presumed that most people know the answer. The announcer and narrator for mystery broadcasts from *Street and Smith's Detective Story Magazine* was characterized in 1930 as The Shadow. The character was so successful that in 1931 Street and Smith began to produce *Shadow Magazine.*

The character was featured in various cameos in the program beginning in 1934, but it was not until the 1936–1937 season that the entire package (as listeners came to know and shudder over) was developed. That package included Lamont Cranston, who had "the ability to cloud men's minds," and Margo Lane.

The Shadow was made into a motion picture in 1940, with Victor Jory playing the leading role. Not a huge number of premiums stemmed from *The Shadow,* as Mr. Cranston was a bit difficult to pin down, but of those that were offered, a couple are quite rare and desirable today.

For most of the period of *The Shadow*'s run (1936–1954), Blue Coal was the sponsor. The Shadow Blue Coal Ring was made of iridescent plastic that glows in the dark. A simulated chunk of Blue Coal was the stone. Today, that ring commands a price of from $80 in good condition to $170 in mint condition. A four-color Blue Coal Ink Blotter will bring up to $15, while a Carey Salt 1947 black stoned Crocodile Ring may command as much as $75. A Shadow Club Stud Pin may bring a price of between $75 and $120.

Alas, the days of anthracite coal as a viable fuel in this country were (then) numbered. While a few other companies attempted to pick up the sponsorship, the voice of the Shadow, as entoned by Orson Welles, was stilled in 1954.

Captain Midnight

In the fall of 1940, following an established trend of radio hero worship, SS-1—as he was known to his intimate friends—went on network radio. The Captain had started as a Skelly Gasoline sponsored re-

Because of their perishability, paper premiums are often worth more than items made of other materials. The Captain Midnight manuals from 1943 to 1949, for example, will bring up to $45 each in mint condition. From those years, only the Mystic Sun-God Ring is worth more.

gional program out of Chicago, but they soon learned that you can't keep a good aviator down. National sponsorship belonged to Ovaltine from 1940 through 1949.

The basic background information on the Captain was provided by Robert Burtt and Willfred Moore—the same writing team that later wrote *Hop Harrigan* and *Sky King*. It told of a daring captain of World War One who had penetrated deep behind enemy lines to complete a mission to save the war. The odds were a hundred to one against his ever succeeding, yet succeed he did, returning home just at the stroke of midnight—hence, his name. Awe inspiring, don't you think? Patsy Donovan was the female interest, replaced by Joyce Ryan during the Ovaltine period. With the aid of his ward, Chuck Ramsey, the dastardly Ivan Shark and his daughter, Fury—as sinister a pair as you could wish to know—were brought to justice.

While not quite as generous to his Secret Squadron members as was Tom Mix to his Straight Shooters, Captain Midnight issued a lot of gear to his faithful followers. Remember, too, he was not on the air for nearly as long as Mix. The first premiums were offered by Skelly Gasoline, before the Secret Squadron even came into being. At that time, the Captain's group was known as the Flight Patrol. Between the end of 1942 and the autumn of 1945, premiums generally were not offered due to a shortage of materials from the war effort. During that period, the program also went off the air for a time.

The Captain Midnight Flight Patrol Membership Medallion of 1940 was gold colored and about the size of a half dollar. On one side was a three bladed propeller with raised heads of the Captain, Chuck Ramsey, and Patsy Donovan between the blades. The other side of the medal had a clock design with the hands pointing straight up to midnight. This medal is worth between $12 and $25 today. An exact replica of this medal, however, is now being offered with the cooperation of the Ovaltine and Skelly companies. A small "R" beneath the S in the Skelly name indicates that this medal is a replica. A membership certificate in the Flight Patrol and a short history of the *Captain Midnight* radio show accompanies this copy which sells for about $3. It is not a bad investment for those interested. Make sure that you get the metal one, though, and not the cardboard duplicate that has been offered by the Longines Symphonette Society.

Another interesting early Flight Patrol premium was a winged badge known as the Mysto-Magic Weather Forecasting Flight Wings.

The Mysto-Magic Weather Fore-
casting Flight Wings were a
Skelly Gasoline premium in 1939.
At about $5, it's a good buy.

To get a Captain Midnight Flight Commander
Flying Cross (1940) now, you may have to come
a-cross with $75.

The original 1940 Flight Patrol
Membership Medallion is still
under $10 and a good investment.

These wings contained a paper insert impregnated with cobalt chloride which turned color from blue to pink when there was high humidity in the air. That way, patrol members could avoid scheduling flights in stormy weather.

Captain Midnight premiums from the Secret Squadron days were possibly the most popular of all premiums from the standpoint of distribution. That was because his equipment, as a general rule, came to the listener absolutely free. Ralston had provided Straight Shooter gear absolutely free in the early days, requesting only a boxtop. I used to send the boxtop for one item, and then the box *bottom* for another. By the forties, however, most shows asked for "proof of purchase," and also demanded "ten cents to cover the cost of postage and handling." Ovaltine, alone, refrained from demanding any expenditure beyond the 3¢ stamp that it cost to mail in the label or inner seal in those days. Remember, though, that a can of Ovaltine, at about sixty cents, cost nearly six times as much as a box of Ralston. It was hard enough back then for many kids to afford the Ovaltine, let alone an additional dime.

When Ovaltine took over sponsorship of *Captain Midnight* in 1940, the most popular of the Captain's premiums came onto the scene. They were naturals, since all children live in their own world, protecting their dreams and secrets from unknown enemies, or parents. Code-O-Graphs were devices to aid in expressing the already known furtive signals that existed to thwart the prying eyes and ears of the grownups. At this period of history, however, the impetus to the success of the decoders was even greater than it might otherwise have been. Real grown-up Nazi and Japanese spies were sending messages to each other on decoders just like Captain Midnight's. Wowee! What fun!!

The *Captain Midnight* radio bulletin set the tone:

> You should be very proud of your membership in Captain Midnight's great organization of young patriotic Americans. We are banded together for a real purpose, helping to guard the future of America. We are opposed to everything that is dishonest, disloyal, and unAmerican! We are pledged to honor the flag, and all that it represents!

Wowee! Now wasn't that super? You might even say "Gee whiz!", if you are prone to injudicious use of expletives. Juvenile patriotism was keyed to a fever pitch, as exemplified by their tuning in—and drinking plenty of Ovaltine.

The two patriotic emblems on the 1941 Mystery Dial Code-O-Graph were the American eagle and the military shield. The code numbers from the broadcast would translate into letters on the decoder. The show would carry an electric air of excitement:

THE SECRET SQUADRON MEETS TONIGHT!
The very air throbs to the roar of the plane in its thundering power dive! That's the signal for red-blooded boys and girls throughout the nation to gather 'round radios for another thrilling adventure with CAPTAIN MIDNIGHT! Every weekday—except Saturday—Captain Midnight is on the air, and he expects every loyal member of his Secret Squadron to be listening in at every meeting.

(Note that a failure to listen in "at every meeting" was a sign of lack of loyalty. Whew! What pressure! If I don't listen in to the Captain, I might be taken for a Nazi spy!)

There will be many important messages broadcast in the Secret Squadron's own secret code! Besides, every member wants to keep up to date on the exciting adventures of Chuck and Joyce in helping Captain Midnight oppose the traitorous plots of Ivan Shark! Never miss a program! Tune in every night for more adventures with *Captain Midnight and the Secret Squadron!!!*

Captain Midnight became so popular that even the government of the United States took an interest in the program as a positive force for morale on the home front. Sheet brass was quite scarce in 1942, yet the Government allocated enough that year to permit the manufacture of the beautifully designed Photomatic Code-O-Graph Decoder Badge. Perhaps the most handsome of all decoders ever offered, the top featured flowing banners bearing the name of our hero. The spinning part of the decoder was made to look like the air-cooled engine of an old Curtiss-Wright six cylinder airplane with a propeller that resembled that of a World War I Spad. Pasted into a half inch square picture frame at the very top was a photograph of Captain Midnight, himself. At last, the man of legend could be seen. In the tiny television-like screen, he was serious faced, wearing flight goggles and a leather flight helmet of the open cockpit type. One of those decoders is worth up to $40 today—if the Captain's picture is still in it. Without our hero's likeness, it's worth no more than $20—unless you happen to have an extra "original" photo stashed away.

The photograph on the 1942 decoder must have been of some square-jawed male model, since it was not a likeness of either Ed Prentiss, who played the Captain on the radio, or of Dave O'Brien, who starred in the motion picture serial.

Disappearing during 1943 and 1944, the Code-O-Graph finally fell victim to the metal shortage produced by wartime. The green metal Lucky Strike package had gone off to war and never returned, but this was not to be the Code-O-Graph's fate. In 1945, they were back again.

The 1945 Magni-Magic Code-O-Graph contained a small magnifying glass in the center. This was of inestimable value when it came to reading messages—especially those that were spelled out in pin-pricks, as the manual recommended. This decoder is worth between $15 and $30 today.

The 1946 version of the decoder was a pin-on badge with a winged star at the top. The words "Captain Midnight's 1946 Secret Squadron" sweep around the dial. On the central knob is a small mirror which could be used to flash messages. This last of the pin-on badges that were offered is worth between $12 and $25 today. The mirror on this decoder is convex, showing a much larger area than would a flat mirror of the same size. That meant that you could keep your eyes on a whole roomful of enemies at the same time while never taking your eyes off your decoder. And, as if that were not swell enough, the code mechanism had become nearly professional in quality. The stationary part was embossed with the letters of the alphabet, while the numerals one through twenty-six were on the rotating disc. That device permitted 676 different code combinations for sending and receiving Secret Squadron messages.

Well, if you think that the 1946 Code-O-Graph was the ultimate—and I certainly did—then neither of us reckoned with its serious deficit! It could not send messages by sound.

Once more into the breach leapt the Mysterious Dr. X, who sat somewhere in his basement in Middle America perfecting the art of Code-O-Graphsmanship. Lo and behold, he produced the 1947 Whistling Code-O-Graph. Basically, it was a red and blue plastic whistle—

Captain Midnight must have pledged to keep his Secret Squadron members in Code-O-Graphs. Except for two years during the war when metal was scarce, they came out annually from 1941 to 1949.

No wonder the F.B.I. wanted this one! It was "Dr. X's" finest hour.

Your Secret KEY-O-MATIC CODE-O-GRAPH

The most amazing instrument Capt. Midnight has ever issued.

Your new, cleverly-designed Key-O-Matic Code-O-Graph, with the very important little key you mustn't lose, serves two vital purposes in your Secret Squadron work.

First—it is your official identification as a member of the new 1949 Secret Squadron, and only those who have this Code-O-Graph are really members. It is exactly like the Code-O-Graph used by Captain Midnight. Note the words "Captain Midnight's S.S.," the date "1949" and the winged insignia embossed on the face of your Code-O-Graph—to mark it as the official identification-piece of the Secret Squadron. The fact that you

have this Code-O-Graph proves to everyone who sees it that you are a member of the Squadron.

Second—with this amazing Key-O-Matic Code-O-Graph you can decode secret messages sent you over the radio by Captain Midnight. You can receive and send secret messages in *676 secret codes*—built from *26 key-codes.* You can change the key-code settings only with your key as shown at the right— and *automatically* decode messages that completely baffle outsiders.

Now that you know the great importance of your Key-O-Matic Code-O-Graph, examine it thoroughly. Note how the case is made of strong durable metal to last a lifetime. Notice its gleaming gold-colored finish and rich decoration. Plan to take care of it carefully. Probably you'll want to tie a string to your Key so it won't get lost easily. And now—you're ready to learn the fascinating secret of Key-O-Matic decoding—by reading the next page.

that's right, plastic. What better testimonial to the old adage that war is hell! Plastic had replaced the metal crafted radio premium.

On the blue side of the whistle was the famous winged midnight insignia, and the figures, SS1947. (Can you decipher the meaning?) The red side contained the dial with the numerals and letters (26 of each). The master key for the day's code was, of course, given by that day's show. Basically it told you what numeral to align with which letter. Sound-signaling was done by means of the longs and shorts of the International Morse Code. The Manual contained the combinations. Most impressive of all, the Code-O-Graph could be used to gauge your enemy's distance.

> Learn to judge distances. Have a friend blow a sharp blast, and wave a handkerchief at the same time. Count the seconds from the instant of the wave until you hear the sound of the whistle. Every second means 1000 feet. If it takes five seconds, the other fellow's 5000 feet—or almost a mile—away from you!

The most amazing device that Captain Midnight ever offered was the 1949 Key-O-Matic Code-O-Graph Decoder. Suddenly, we were back to the shiny brass case, but inside . . . Wow, what was inside that case! There was a set of plastic gears that were carefully calibrated with the usual 26 letters and 26 numerals set into each gear. Dr. X had completely outdone himself. Only one numeral and one letter showed at a time through two tiny windows in the brass case. As you turned the gear wheel at the bottom with your thumb, both the numeral and the letter would change. In order to alter the operant code, a key had to be inserted and used as follows:

HOW TO SET YOUR CAPTAIN MIDNIGHT CODE-O-GRAPH
FOR KEY CODES

Keep turning until you see the number you want. For example, let's imagine you want 6, for Key Code B-6. Keep your Code-O-Graph set with number 6 showing. Now put your key in the two small openings near the top of your Code-O-Graph—beneath the letters S.S. Push down on the key and hold it down. You will then find that you can turn the red wheel WITHOUT CHANGING THE NUMBER—only the letters change. Now turn the red wheel until the letter you want shows in the opening—in this case letter

B. Then take out the key. You now have set your Code-O-Graph
for Key Code B-6 and are ready to start decoding any message in
Key Code B-6 automatically.

Do not lose the very important little key. Tie a string to your
key so that it won't get lost easily.

The story goes that the Key-O-Matic Code-O-Graph Decoder was
so advanced that Ovaltine received a request for samples from the Federal Bureau of Investigation. Perhaps they feared that the Russians
might get hold of one. Perhaps the Russians did! It would be fascinating to learn whether today there remains a file on Captain Midnight in
some drawer at the K.G.B. or the C.I.A. A known fact is that no decoders were produced after this last one, and the mysterious Dr. X was
never heard from again. Kinda makes you wonder . . .

Valuable and sought after as the Code-O-Graphs are, still more valuable are the manuals that went with them. A Key-O-Matic is worth
from $10 to over $20 today, but the 1949 Manual is worth twice as
much. Now maybe you'll remember not to throw away the instructions
so cavalierly . . . next time.

Ovaltine shake-up mugs and insignia badges, rings, and patches
abound from the *Captain Midnight* show. The Mystic Sun God Ring of
1945 commands up to $75 on today's market. Nearly everyone who has
ever heard of the program swears that one premium offered was a Secret Decoder Ring. Exhaustive research, however, has failed to turn up
that particular premium. Is it possible that the only remaining one is in
your trunk?

Have you heard the news? The news about that marvelous
new two piece, bright colored Shake-Up Mug that Captain Midnight has for you? That big, handsome two-in-one shaker-upper
you use to make ice cold chocolaty shake-ups to drink every day?
Well sir, Captain Midnight has one for you *almost as a gift.*

You can't buy one in the stores at any price. They're patented,
and made only for Captain Midnight and his Ovaltine-drinking
pals. Why, if we sold one to an outsider, our regular price for this
big, handsome, two-piece Shake-Up Mug would be fifty cents,
but *you* can have one for just fifteen cents and the label from
your jar of Ovaltine. . . .

How is that for the ultimate in commercial exploitation? It was dia-
bolically ingenious. The sponsor got you to spend your money on his

What use is a 1945 Mystic Sun-God Ring if you don't know how to use its secret compartment?

The year was 1955. The premium was red and it had a blue top. Can you guess what it is? (The answer will shake you up.)

product so that you could spend more money to get an item that would help you to use more of his product. Moreover, kids loved shaking up a mug full of Ovaltine, because they were convinced—theoretically—that it was like making "a creamy milkshake." Why, it was just like having a soda fountain right there in their own home. Personally, I never did care for the taste of Ovaltine, but I gritted my teeth long enough to get my mug. Then I used Bosco in it.

The Ovaltine Shake-Up Mug could well be called the most durable premium of the entire radio era. It lasted throughout the entire era, in fact. Captain Midnight's version was a red plastic cup with a blue cap. The first mug Ovaltine offered, however, was an Uncle Wiggily Mug, and that was before the days of commercial broadcasting. Little Orphan Annie offered her mug in 1930 (for the first time), until 1940 when Captain Midnight took over. It was the last of his radio premiums (1950), and was also offered on his television program. Another Shake-Up Mug was offered by Ovaltine in connection with the mid 1960's Olympic Games. Today, grownups are willing to pay up to $35 to recapture the youthful pleasure of shaking up their Ovaltine.

The Green Hornet

The Green Hornet came from a long line of staunch defenders of justice. Bret Reid was born (first broadcast) in 1936. He was descended from another masked avenger of the airwaves:

> "Dad," Bret Reid said to his father, Dan, "I know personally that the Green Hornet is no criminal. In his own way he fights for law and order. Can you believe that?"
> Old Dan Reid nodded his gray head slowly. "I think I know what you are trying to tell me."
> The young publisher met the eyes of the man who had built the *Daily Sentinel* into one of America's greatest newspapers. "Dad, I am the Green Hornet!"
> "I suspected as much," the elder Reid said.
> "How could you? The world thinks I am nothing but an idle playboy, dabbling in the newspaper business."
> "Son, you've seen the painting on this wall many times. I gave it to you years ago."

"Why yes, Dad—the picture of the Masked Man on the great white horse."

"Everyone knows who he was. But the world does not know that the Masked Man is your ancestor, Bret; my uncle and your great uncle."

And there you have it. Like the Lone Ranger before him, the Green Hornet wore a mask. Instead of a great white horse, Silver, he had a powerful limousine, Black Beauty, and Kato was to the Green Hornet what Tonto was to his ancestor.

During the middle 1930's, it was George W. Trendle's intention to put the Masked Rider of the Plains into a more contemporary setting. Fran Striker and the rest of the creative staff at Detroit's station WXYZ wrote both shows, and, reportedly, Striker preferred the second.

The Green Hornet apparently offered only one premium from its beginning in 1936 until it ended its run in 1952. Ah, but what a premium that was. The Secret Compartment Glow-in-the-Dark Green Hornet Seal Ring—even the name was a douzey— of 1947 was one of the most attractive and complicated of all radio premiums. Not only did it glow in the dark (what didn't in 1947?), but the round front was an embossed brass seal that could be used with hot wax to seal envelopes containing secret messages. The Green Hornet used his ring to imprint his hornet seal on the forehead of a criminal who fell to his gas gun's relentless power. Then he would fade into the night to meet the faithful Kato at Black Beauty and return to his office at the *Daily Sentinel.*

That ring that you sent away for was perfect for imprinting your school composition book, and the secret compartment would hold just enough money for a Hershey Bar—with almonds. Today, your ring would be worth between $80 and $120.

Tarzan of the Apes

Tarzan was far more successful as a comic strip and motion picture character than he was on the air. When the show first aired in 1932, the roles of Jane and Tarzan were played by none other than Edgar Rice Burroughs' daughter Joan and his son-in-law, James Pierce. The series was on three times a week, and was syndicated in a number of markets.

*The Green Hornet offered
a ring in 1947. What
a ring! It had a
secret compartment,
glowed in the dark,
and could seal messages.
It could cost you $120 today.*

*Don't sneeze at a Sergeant Preston of the Yukon
membership button. It can bring up to $40.*

*Here it is! The deed to one
square inch of land in the
Yukon Gold Territory. Gosh!*

*You can't find your gold claim without your map of the Yukon Territory. It's
worth nearly twice as much as the deed.*

*Sergeant Preston had a pedometer, too.
He used it to keep track of how far he
mushed.*

There were many different sponsors. Noodles, milk, and coffee show up on various premiums, linking the ape-man with those products.

The series was faithful to the Edgar Rice Burroughs' books, and to the comic strips. As the networks formed, though, the audience for the syndicated show's episodes diminished, until they were finally withdrawn in 1936. Some premiums came from the original go-round, mostly in the form of badges bearing Tarzan's likeness along with messages such as "Drink More Milk," or "Bursley Coffees." These badges will fetch from $20 to $65 today. There was also a Girl's Bracelet with the inscription "Tarzan Radio Club DRINK MORE MILK" offered in 1934. That is worth up to $70.

A number of statues of Tarzan characters were offered by Fould's Noodle Products, the most sought after now is that of our hero himself. The Tarzan statue is worth between $10 and $23. The other figures, including Numa the Lion, Kala the Ape Mother, Jane, and The Witch Doctor, are worth from $3 to $17.

The show made a second try at syndication in 1951, and ran for one more year (1952) after CBS took it over. As far as is known, there are no premiums in existence from the show's second time around.

Sergeant Preston of the Yukon

Sergeant Preston was a late comer to the radio waves. He first aired in 1947, and the official name of the show was *The Challenge of the Yukon.* Actually, the show had been kicking around as a serial for years, but it was not until Quaker Puffed Wheat picked it up in 1947 that it made any kind of a national splash. The sponsor had selected it to replace the serialized *Terry and the Pirates* at a time when the half-hour complete show format was becoming popular. Wisely, they went to good old George W. Trendle, who assured the show's success.

Special pocket size editions of comic books, packed inside boxes of Quaker Puffed Wheat and Quaker Puffed Rice, told us how Preston came to be a Mountie and how he found his wonder dog, Yukon King. These books are worth from $3 to $7 apiece now. They were ideal premiums, because they were basically samples of the radio show itself.

Of course, Sergeant Preston also offered us a police whistle, just like the one that he used to summon Yukon King, and with his very own signature on it, too. The whistle, issued in 1949, will bring from $8 to $15 nowadays.

Probably the most exciting offer ever made on radio, though, belonged to the Sergeant. It was a deed to one square inch (count it, one) of land in the Yukon gold territory. A recent investigation by a collector has shown that these deeds have since expired—a great disappointment to me, for one. I should have thought that the good Sergeant would have had a greater interest in protecting his credibility for all time. On the other hand, maybe he didn't really let us down after all. How many land deeds do you know of have appreciated *seventeen thousand percent* in thirty years—and without even being negotiable for the land! That's right, from 10¢, a deed to a square inch of the Yukon is worth up to $17 today.

CHAPTER IV

Buck Rogers in the 25th Century

No matter how you look at it, Mr. Rogers is worth a buck in any century. It all began with the August, 1928, issue of *Amazing Stories*. The beginning went like this:

> Elsewhere I have set down, for whatever interest they have in this, the 25th Century, my personal recollections of the 20th Century.
>
> Now it occurs to me that my memoirs of the 25th Century may have an equal interest 500 years from now, particularly in view of the unique perspective from which I have seen the 25th Century, entering it as I did, in one leap across a gap of 492 years.
>
> I should state therefore, that I, Anthony Rogers, am, so far as I know, the only man alive whose normal span of eighty-one years of life has been spread over a period of 573 years. To be precise, I lived the first twenty-nine years of my life between 1898 and 1927; the other fifty-two since 2419. The gap between these two, a period of nearly five hundred years, I spent in a state from the ravages of katabolic processes, and without any apparent effect on my physical or mental faculties.
>
> When I began my long sleep, man had just begun his real conquest of the air in a sudden series of trans-oceanic flights in airplanes driven by internal combustion motors. He had barely begun to speculate on the possibilities of harnessing sub-atomic forces, and had made no further practical penetration into the field of ethereal pulsations than the primitive radio and television of that day. The United States of America was the most powerful nation in the world, its political, financial, industrial and scientific influence being supreme; and in the arts also it was climbing into leadership.

I awoke to find the America I knew a total wreck—to find
Americans a hunted race in their own land, hiding in the dense
forests that covered the shattered and leveled ruins of their once
magnificent cities, desperately preserving, and struggling to de-
velop in their secret retreats the remnants of their culture and
science . . .

I shall pass over the days of mental agony that followed in my
attempt to grasp the meaning of it all. There were times that I felt
that I was on the verge of insanity. I roamed the unfamiliar forest
like a lost soul. Had it not been for the necessity of improvising
traps and crude clubs with which to slay my food, I believe I
should have gone mad. Suffice to say, however, that I survived
this psychic crisis. I shall begin my narrative proper with my first
contact with Americans of the year 2419 A.D.

> "Armageddon—2419 A.D."
> by Philip Francis Nowlan

The fantastic firing of fans' imaginations that followed Rogers' introduction to the world was just at its kindling stage. An industry
based upon outer space was launched at the depth of the worst depression in the history of the United States. It was to make millionaires
of people who made comic strips, movie serials, radio programs, not to
mention those who specialized in radio premiums—wrist watches,
printing sets, model casting sets, games, space suits, roller skates that
looked like rocket ships, and a host of related manufactured novelties.

When *Amazing Stories* added two full-size illustrations with three
cartoon panels to the story, Nowlan came up with the idea of submit-
ting his character and concept to a comic strip syndicate. In 1929, the
president of the National Newspaper Syndicate of America, John F.
Dille, agreed to change Nowlan's character into a comic strip hero. It
was Dille who decided to change Anthony Rogers' name to Buck—a
decision which was greeted with a good deal of opposition, since most
of his associates thought that Buck Rogers sounded more like a cowboy than a space hero.

In January, 1929, the first strip appeared, sporting the title, "Buck
Rogers 2429 A.D." Each year, the title of the strip was to be updated by
a year, so as to keep the 500 year differential. As the character grew in
popularity, the name of the strip was changed to "Buck Rogers in the
25th Century."

The comic strip added new words to the English language, many of which are still in use today. Futuristic inventions proliferated. There were rocket pistols, rocket ships which traveled at thousands of miles per hour, flying belts, television, weightlessness, and disintegrators.

Years later, many of the inventions first introduced as far out Buck Rogers' equipment came into being. The lie detector, nuclear submarine, spy satellite, space suit, space laboratory, atomic power plant and bombs, and even the instant picture camera were ideas popularized by the comic strip.

While Philip Nowlan continued to write Buck Rogers, and Dick Calkins, John Dille's best staff cartoonist, drew the famous characters of Buck, his girlfriend Wilma Deering, and scientist par excellence Dr. Huer, not to mention the villainous Killer Kane, Ardala, and a plethora of weird monsters and machines, Dille kept supplying most of the futuristic inventions. Many of John Dille's friends were University of Chicago faculty members, connected to the science department. Combined with Dille's having sent his son to that institution, there was a constant source of plausible futuristic ideas flowing from what was to become the seat of the first nuclear chain reaction.

Between 1929 and 1967, the year it finally ended, the Buck Rogers comic strip succeeded beyond all expectations. It had been translated into eighteen languages, and appeared in approximately 450 newspapers. Ray Bradbury, the exceptional science fiction writer, recalling his youth wrote:

"The most beautiful sound in my life was the sound of a folded newspaper kiting through the air landing on my front porch.

"Every afternoon from the time I was nine until I was fourteen that sound, and the thump it made hitting the side of the house, or the screen door, or a window, but never the porch planks themselves, that sound had an immediate effect upon one person inside the house.

"The door burst wide. A boy, myself, leapt out, eyes blazing, mouth gasping for breath, hands seizing at the paper to grapple it wide so that the hungry soul of one of Waukegan, Illinois' finest small intellects could feed upon:

BUCK ROGERS IN THE 25TH CENTURY!

"... his first, my first, huge mania. ... And I gave away my Buck Rogers collection!

"My Buck Rogers collection! Which was like giving away my head, my heart, my soul, and half a lung. I walked wounded for a year after

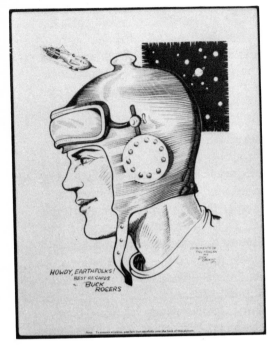

Buck Rogers fans eagerly sent for photos of their hero

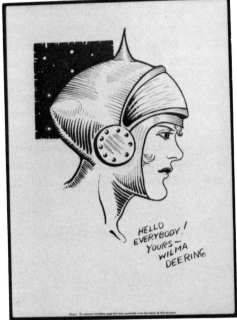

. . . and heroine.

The Buck Rogers Chief Explorer Badge was an early Cream of Wheat premium.

In 1934, Buck "zapped 'em" with this futuristic Rocket Pistol.

that. I grieved and cursed myself for having so dumbly tossed aside what was, in essence, the greatest love of my life."

Ah, what a collection that might have been! With the exception of Mickey Mouse, no other comic character offered such an abundant variety of exquisite collectibles. All of them exhibited influences of Art Deco and Art Nouveau elements liberally sprinkled in with futuristic motifs of twenty-fifth century space monsters and fantastic machinery. The unique artistic style of the comic strip was sculpted into three dimensional surrealism.

Licensed by the John F. Dille Company, a fortune was earned during the worst years of the Depression just from royalties on the premiums and toys. The years of comic strip and radio broadcast exposure that preceded the introduction of the first merchandise assured virtually instantaneous commercial success. The publicity groundwork had been laid well in advance. The first strip had appeared January 7, 1929. The first Buck Rogers radio show was broadcast on November 7, 1932. The first Buck Rogers merchandise, however, did not appear on the market until 1933. Then, many of the items were worked into the radio shows and the comics in order to create specific demand for the products.

The XZ-31 Buck Rogers Rocket Pistol, the first of seven different pistols marketed under Buck's aegis, was the toy success of 1934. Made of heavy gauge blued gun steel and trimmed with nickel plating, it was 9½ inches long and made a loud "zzzap" when fired. It was the same gun that was seen every Sunday in the comics, and added the transitive verb, *zap,* to the American language. Costing a whopping nickel to produce, it sold at leading department stores for a half a buck. The colorful carton was covered with scary space creatures and space ships, and the gun's muzzle was shown shooting out a fiery "Zap–Zap–Zap."

The XZ-31 Rocket Pistol was produced by the Daisy Manufacturing Company. Daisy, in fact, produced all seven of the guns. Since 1935 was not exactly a year of affluence in this country, the same pistol was remanufactured that year to a length of 7½ inches, packed in a smaller carton, and renamed the XZ-35. The XZ-35 retailed for a quarter. Since both the XZ-31 and XZ-35 were as well made as real weapons, they can still be easily restored to mint condition by the collector, or for the collector by any gunsmith.

The rocket pistol shown in the comic strip bore a striking resem-

Buck Rogers' arsenal was made available to Solar Scouts—and others—by the Daisy Manufacturing Company.

This Buck Rogers Map of the Solar System is a Cocomalt premium circa 1934. In mint condition, it's worth up to $200.

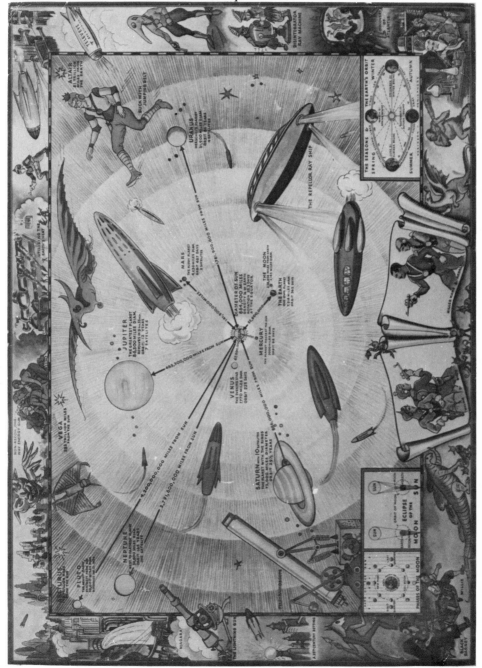

blance to an automatic, except that it had a much larger magazine. Of course, it had a much longer range than an ordinary pistol, and the bullet was highly explosive. The propelling charge and its case traveled with the bullet instead of remaining in the gun, thereby imparting a much flatter trajectory to the missile which, it must be duly recorded, had an explosive power equal to a twentieth century heavy artillery shell. Can you imagine the power that possession of this weapon gave to any child with a knowledge of the comic strip and a modicum of imagination?

Depending upon its condition, and the hungriness of the collector, an XZ-31 or XZ-35 today will bring a minimum of $40 to anyone mercenary enough to part with one. There is no top figure possible to set, for how can anyone put a price on such a powerful force?

In May, 1935, the American Toy Show in New York City was the scene of the first public showing of a new concept in futuristic weaponry: the XZ-38 Buck Rogers Disintegrator Pistol. It was completely different in design and operation from the Rocket Pistols. Made of copper, it had an "electronic compression viewplate" which was lit up by a secret ray within every time the gun was fired.

> The process of disintegration of buildings, aircraft, and people who get in Buck Rogers' way is accomplished by an electronic barrage created within the gun by means of an electronic compression chamber and a sub-atomic condenser discharged by an impulse generator controlled by a beam intensity selector and aimed by a disintegration beam director. Of course, as the electronic discharge leaves the gun, the barrel under normal circumstances would become very hot. Not in the Buck Rogers disintegrator, however, for the barrel is cooled by a tri-thermal convergence unit.

Needless to say, with all the guns that were on the market in the 1930's, it was essential that a holster be provided if any new weapon was to have a chance of commercial success. Since Daisy was a quality manufacturer, the holster that they provided was of thick black leather—remember that stuff? This ensured that most disintegrators would remain in top-notch condition, and may be found so even to today.

The most eye-catching Buck Rogers pistol ever designed came from the Daisy gun-works in 1936. It was the XZ-44 Buck Rogers 25th Century Liquid Helium Water Pistol. Capable of being fired fifteen times without reloading, it was finished in brilliant red and yellow. It was succeeded by a model finished in copper, but that later model just didn't make the same statement.

The aftermath of World War Two brought with it an intense fascination with atomic energy. No wonder, then, that the U-235 Atomic Pistol was an instantaneous success when introduced in 1946. It was made with the same tools and dies that had effected the 1936 Disintegrator Pistol. The U-238 Atomic Pistol of 1948 was the same gun, but with a holster.

So successful was Daisy's experience with the Buck Rogers pistols, that other manufacturers gained the courage to enter the market. Louis Marx submitted sketches to John Dille and obtained the rights to produce a Buck Rogers 25th Century Rocket Ship. Sears Roebuck included it in their catalog, and ran this ad in local newspapers:

> Buck Rogers 25th Century Rocket Ship! The toy sensation of 1934! Special 78¢ Wednesday only.
> It flashes with a trail of sparks and a weird droning sound. Colorful lithography. Wing protected wheels. Powerful windup spring. Replaceable protected flint shoots the sparks. Heavy gauge metal; 12 inches long. Extra flint included.

Buck Rogers and Dr. Huer could be seen through one side cockpit window, while through the other side Buck and Wilma Deering were visible. Fins, wings, turrets, and rocket tubes completed the spaceworthy craft.

The collectibles of the Buck Rogers line were truly works of art. They were designs of comic art made expressly for the characters that they purported to be for. They were not surplus stock dressed up with a pretty paint job to help move the items (as became the case with the post World War II items). Cheap Depression wages coupled with the efforts of comic artists, toy designers, tool makers, and precariously secured bank loans made possible truly unique and beautiful creations, many of which have gained with each passing decade still greater acceptance as artistic achievements.

The Marx Company's roller skates are truly museum pieces. Made

If you owned this badge in 1936, it proved you were a member of the Solar Scouts. Now it proves you are a collector.

The Flight Commander Whistle Badge (1935) is worth up to $50 today.

No Solar Scout should be without a Buck Rogers pen-knife. This 1935 premium would run about $75 today, in mint condition.

The Buck Rogers All-Fair Card Game had a colorful cast of characters—human and otherwise. Buck's initials are prominent in the design on the backs of the cards.

*This stand-up figure of Wilma Deering is from a Cut-Out Buck Rogers Adventure Book. In mint condition—**intact**—you could ask, and get, $230 for the book.*

Six Bucktoys given out to Solar Scouts were also stand-ups.

Buck Rogers merchandise is still easy to find.

of heavy gauge quality steel, they were shaped like rocketships. The rear of each skate sported bicycle-type red reflectors to simulate the flames coming from the rockets' tails.

Daisy manufactured two Buck Rogers Helmets. Sackman Brothers of New York developed the Buck Rogers and Wilma Deering playsuits for boys and girls. Then, together, the two companies marketed a set that consisted of the following: a two-piece orange and black jersey shirt with a picture of Buck in a leather medallion, his hand clutching his rocket pistol; suedine leggings and britches; an official suedine helmet; and an official Buck Rogers pistol and leather holster. Packaged in a large box and sold in sizes 4 to 14, the entire outfit retailed for $4.50 in 1934 in leading department stores, or it could be gotten from the radio sponsors for Cream of Wheat boxtops.

Casting kits for sculpting, in lead, models of the heroes, villains, and rockets came in three sizes: electric, midget, and junior. All the sets carried directions and materials for casting the figures and for painting them. They ranged in price from $1.50 to $3.50. Teiko men, Mekkano men, Depth men, and Disintegrator machines were also available, either as parts of sets or as extra molds to be purchased separately. The popularity of these kits can be traced to the sales pitch that was particularly well geared to the years of the Depression.

Thousands of kids convinced their parents that a Buck Rogers Casting Set was not just a toy, but an investment. The pitch was that anyone could start his or her own toy business by painting their castings and then selling them "at great profit." Kids started selling each other the painted figures of Buck's 25th Century world. In fact, there are still people who are casting the figures and making side money at flea markets and antique get-togethers.

The R.B. Davis Company, makers of a chocolate flavored drink called Cocomalt, sponsored the Buck Rogers radio show when it went on the air, and a torrent of radio premiums followed. One of the most sought after premiums among collectors today is Cocomalt's Buck Rogers Map of the Solar System. It contains drawings of the solar system and Buck in his flying belt. The "real" Buck Rogers radio cast, in outer space costumes, are depicted also, along with a host of monsters, rocketships, meteors, and machines.

Kellogg's, Cream of Wheat, and later Popsicle and Post Toasties also were sponsors of the show, each company adding successively to the collection of premiums. Three Art Deco badges—Solar Scout,

Chief Explorer, and Space Commander—were issued by Cream of Wheat. An offered Wilma Deering Medallion was gold plated and came with a sixteen inch gold chain. One of the most sought after premiums among collectors today, it carries a profile view of Wilma in her space helmet, and the back is inscribed: "To my pals in the Solar Scouts."

Of course, there was also the ever popular radio ring. The Buck Rogers Secret Repeller Ray Seal Ring showed Buck seated in his open air rocket sled, with the repeller, a green stone, imbedded in the side of the ship. It was used to seal all secret correspondence, and was later replaced by the Ring of Saturn which was made of the ubiquitous plastic that glowed in the dark.

It would be possible to go on like this for pages and pages more, and yet it is not necessary to do so in order to get to the point of it all. Buck Rogers is a trip unto himself. One could collect nothing but Buck Rogers memorabilia and still amass a collection of massive proportions. There were literally dozens of items manufactured in large production runs to immortalize the hero of the 25th Century. Continuous searching can lead to the discovery of additional Buck Rogers memorabilia as yet unearthed. There is a considerable market right now for recordings of the radio program made after the beginning of the Second World War. The programs from before the war were recorded on discs and, to date, none has been found. Imagine what a coup it would be to unearth one or more of them!

Acquiring Tarzan or Flash Gordon items, not to mention the Shadow or Green Hornet, would lead to a collection of quite limited scope, inasmuch as not very many items were manufactured for these characters. Buck, on the other hand, captured the world's imagination, and the variety of collectibles available with the 25th Century motif demonstrates that fact. The rarest of the Buck Rogers items still known to exist is original art from 1929 through 1940. Most of these black ink on white cardboard comic strip drawings were burned by one of the artists associated with the strip nineteen years ago. What remains is worth thousands of dollars to every wealthy collector, and most museums.

CHAPTER V

A Mixed Bag of Tricks

Virtually all the radio shows that really made it big in the premium grab-bag were mystery and adventure shows of one form or another. Western or futuristic, superhero or spy, it was generally the show's ability to maintain some degree of suspense that kept the listener tuning in night after night, year after year. There were exceptions, of course, such as comedy shows of the Jack Benny or Fred Allen variety.

Amos 'n' Andy

Amos 'n' Andy was one big exception. The show ran for twenty seven years and was so popular that movie theatres used to schedule their performances so that the intermission would fall when the radio show was on. The broadcast would then be piped in to the audience, so that

Perhaps nobody's perfect, but Amos 'n' Andy's song was.

people could attend the movies and still not miss a single fifteen minute episode. Still, it remained primarily the adventure shows which created the type of cult that premiums appealed to.

Amos 'n' Andy's 27-year run began in 1929, and it had become a national institution by 1931. Only five premiums are known to have been offered during that entire run, and of those the most valued today are the 1930 stand-up *cardboard* figures, which will fetch up to $75 today. (One reason why paper premiums are so valuable is that paper contains an acid that causes the material to self destruct within 50 years. Then again, the material is not known to survive very long in normal day-to-day (ab)use.)

Radio Orphan Annie

Little Orphan Annie does not fit neatly into any single category of show. *Annie* was the first afternoon radio adventure serial that counts. It was also the first "kids" show to last more than a few seasons. The "chatterbox with pretty auburn locks" was, naturally enough, the first to offer a premium. While the record is not completely clear on what that first premium was, it seems to be a pretty good bet that it was an Ovaltine Shake-Up Mug. If, in fact, that was not the first, then it should have been.

The makers of Ovaltine, The Wander Company, lifted Annie from her rather staid life on the comics pages of the *Chicago Tribune* and put her on the airwaves in 1930. The first version, out of Chicago, featured Shirley Bell as the waif. Another version, a little later, originated in San Francisco and starred Floy Margaret Hughes.

Annie's early adventures took place around Simmons Corners. New characters such as Joe Corntassel and Ma and Pa Silo, who had never been in the comic strip, were added. Annie stuck pretty much to playmates her own age, and Daddy Warbucks who had made a fortune in munitions (war-bucks!) was not around very often. When he was, he was a considerably mellower fellow than the comic strip protagonist who had created a private army with his wealth and used to go around killing anybody who got in the way of his aspirations.

Leapin' Lizards, Annie's radio adventures were exciting! Annie and Joe might get lost in the woods one afternoon, and be rescued from a fiery haystack another. The inanity of it all was enough to drive any-

The 1936 Silver Star Ring bore the crossed keys symbol of Annie's Secret Society. It should not be confused with the 1938 Silver Star Triple Mystery Secret Compartment Ring.

Do you remember Orphan Annie's Song? For $5 to $9, you can buy the 1931 sheet music.

The Orphan Annie Face Ring was offered in 1934.

What wouldn't you give to own a complete collection of Radio Orphan Annie Decoders (1935 through 1940) like this one?

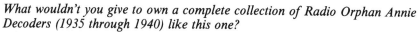

The secret message on the 1937 Radio Orphan Annie Silver Star Secret Message Ring reads (in numbers): "I am a Silver Star Member of Orphan Annie's Secret Society and belong to the circle of her special friends."

Now, wouldn't you like to wear this beautiful mask? Given away free in 1933, today it could cost you $25.

Nobody who walks on the sunny side of the street should be without a 1933 Radio Orphan Annie Sun Watch.

Look sharp and you're likely to spot Radio Orphan Annie collectibles anywhere.

one to drink, so that an Ovaltine Shake-Up Mug was a natural. Daddy Warbucks became essential to give the show a bit more appeal to the urban audience.

During one of Big Daddy's periods of guardianship, he took Annie and Joe on a trip to the South Pacific. Marooned on an island crammed with hostile savages, our heroes took refuge in an old abandoned fort(!). Ingenious as she was, Annie got out her pad and crayons and drew many likenesses of herself with circular face, circular eyes without pupils, and red squiggly hair. She put one of those pictures in every empty window and gunport in the fort so that when the natives attacked, one look at the formidable opposition caused them to flee in panic—all hope abandoned. "Never overestimate your ignorant savage" appears to have been the moral of this episode.

As if that wasn't enough, soon a paper likeness of her face was offered as a premium to the waiting world.

Whether or not you were aware of it, it was Annie who popularized decoder badges. Beginning in 1935, she offered a new one each year. The 1935 decoder was not particularly well designed, nor interesting to operate, but by 1936, she was distributing pure Art Deco.

The 1936 decoder served three functions. First, pinned on your sweater, it proved to all the other kids in the neighborhood that you were a *Radio Orphan Annie Secret Society* member. Its secret compartment carried messages and money (both provided by you) and, last but certainly not least, it automatically decoded secret transmissions. The year, "1936," is deeply embossed on the top of the decoder, in solid brass. Today, that badge would make a really "in" brooch. No matter how you look at it, it's a bargain at from $8 to $12.

By 1938, Annie had achieved national prominence as the president of the Secret Society. Vice-president Joe Corntassel was played by Mel Torme, the singer. That year was also the occasion for the issuance of a star-shaped decoder pin, a full two inches in diameter. No outsider would ever suspect that it was a decoder, since the mechanism was hidden from view, and only two windows on the outside revealed the hidden numerals and letters. That decoder bore the Mysterious Crossed Keys that were to become the Secret Salute. The Secret Handshake included gently pressing your thumb against the hand of the person you suspected might be an ally, and then seeing whether he pressed your hand exactly five times in return. It was the show's fifth anniversary (networkwise), and that was a very big deal. If the person did not return your five presses, then he was " . . . an outsider, and doesn't really understand what you are doing at all!" That was also the year of the Silver Star Triple Mystery Secret Compartment Ring (which is now worth about $40).

The most sought after of all *Orphan Annie* premiums is a pinlever wrist watch with a thirty hour movement from New Haven. The watch had a chrome case and leather strap, and was offered in 1934 for $2.65. By 1939, the price had zoomed to $2.98. Today, that watch will easily bring $145.

There was also an electric miniature stove that really worked (now worth $30), and a whole bunch of household items (salt and pepper shakers, dishes, etc.) which are among the better collectibles of today.

In 1940, the Ovaltine people decided that the world was more interested in a contemporary aviator than in a street waif, so they gave up sponsorship of *Annie* and took off with *Captain Midnight*. Up until that time, the show had been written by Ovaltine's Chicago advertising agency. Although sponsorship was picked up by Quaker Puffed Wheat Sparkies, to all intents and purposes, the age of *Orphan Annie* on the airwaves was over. There were, however, more premiums issued by Sparkies; some of these are detailed in the price guide chapter.

Jack Armstrong

The All-American Boy hit the premium trail in 1933, and spent an awfully long time trying to get his diploma from Hudson High. Among the premiums that he offered was probably one of the most appropriate in the entire history of radio—a sound effects kit. Among other things, the kit contained red cellophane which you could crinkle to make the sound of a crackling fire. The red color of the cellophane is just one more indication that the radio people had ethics. (A green fire would never do.) A balloon with a pebble inside it was ideal for creating the roll of thunder that might accompany ominous clouds upon the horizon. It was unfortunate that the 200 watt audio amplifier which might have added a good deal more realism to these effects was missing, but, then again, kids generally supplied a good deal of detail with their imaginations. That 1937 Sound Effects Kit is worth about $40 today.

Jack Armstrong had many adventures, from which stemmed many of the premiums that he offered. A wise Tibetan lama once gave Jack a

Tom Mix? Gene Autry? No, it's Jack Armstrong, the All-American Boy, on his trusty steed Blackster.

The All-American Boy rarely made a decision in 1938 without consulting his Magic Answer Box.

What do you suppose Jack Armstrong ate for breakfast? He was a champion, you'll recall.

The ideal radio premium. Jack was always thinking.

Jack Armstrong's Secret Bombsight was offered in 1935. It's worth more than $100 now in mint condition—with all three bombs.

Magic Answer Box that would "suggest" an answer to any question that was asked of it. A dial on the little red box permitted a range of mystical answers such as "yes," "no," and "perhaps." A cellophane strip was made to expand and push an arrow to the correct answer by the heat of the user's thumb. With this "ouija board," you too could solve the mysteries of the universe in the very same way that wise Tibetan lamas did.

Jack's offer of a plastic "Iron Key" was a trailblazing device in the art of radio premiumdom. This legendary key played a significant role in unravelling an adventure that took place in far-off India. The significance of the key—its true significance, that is—is that it glowed in the dark. Someday, it will be difficult to find a radio premium that did *not* glow in the dark.

Another incredible adventure—this time to exotic Egypt—brought forth yet one more portent of things to come. It was an Egyptian ring with a spinning siren-whistle on top. Many premiums that came later contained spinning siren-whistles in arrowheads, badges, and ends of pens.

A rather amusing incident concerns a luminous ring with carvings of crocodiles on the band. They hold the stone in their jaws. Jack picked up this goody on a trip to the Sulu Sea, and the people at Wheaties must have really gotten carried away when they placed their order with the novelty manufacturer. A series of recordings of the show from this period reveal announcer Franklyn McCormack growing increasingly frantic each time he made the pitch for the crocodile ring. Just picture the General Mills' warehouses bulging with crocodile rings and having no room to hold any Wheaties or Cheerios.

Finally, listeners were being urged to send for *two* rings, so that you might wear one on each hand and give the impression of two tiger eyes glowing in the dark.

Jack Armstrong started off as a fifteen minute serial about a traditionally idealized high school hero who—through his optimistic approach to life—helped many youths cope with the tribulations of the Great Depression. As times improved, so did Jack's budget, causing his adventures to take on a worldwide scope by the middle to late 1930's. He spent most of the war years outsmarting spies and saboteurs—with which the home front literally teemed.

It was in 1947 that Jack went to a complete half-hour show format, bidding farewell to his "Uncle Jim," and joining—along with his inseparable friends, Betty and Billy Fairfield—the Scientific Bureau of Investigation. Soon, the show was renamed *Armstrong of the SBI*. Of course, Vic Hardy, Jack's nominal boss at the S.B.I., had a higher rank, so Jack was basically placed in a back seat. In the thirteen years that it had taken Jack to get through high school, this was his first serious blunder. Just as *Radio Orphan Annie* had suffered from taking a back seat to Captain Sparks, Jack suffered too. His audience dwindled until finally, in 1951, the show was forced to depart for the great studio in the sky.

World War Two premiums were always tinged with a militaristic flavor. A boxtop could bring you cardboard models of fighting airplanes that at a later time would be available on the backs of cereal boxes. McCormack was almost accusative when he asked: "Have you gotten your Japanese Zero or Grumman Hellcat yet?" That was one of the very few times that "hell" was ever heard over the air.

The Jack Armstrong Norden Bombsight was another premium that certainly smacked of the temper of the times (not to mention the *News, Mirror,* and *Journal-American*). This wooden box let you look down on cardboard cutouts of enemy ships below, through an arrangement of mirrors. Then, when you had them all lined up, these little red bombs could wipe them all out. Kids had loads of fun killing hundreds of thousands of the enemy. Wowee! Just think of how we were molding their awarenesses.

Once Jack joined the S.B.I., the show became readily forgettable. He was no longer that All-American boy whom we had grown to know and love. As a federal agent, Jack Armstrong did not offer so much as a kit for bugging enemy agents' telephones. He had come a long way— down—since the early days, and he apparently did not want to leave any memorabilia by which his waning years might be perpetuated.

Probably the premium most closely identified with Jack Armstrong was his Pedometer. This *amazing, scientifically designed, sturdily constructed* instrument could keep track of every step that you took. All you had to do was to hang it on your belt, and it would count every step that you took on your hike into the great outdoors. You could "have your gang guess how far it is to the camping ground," and then use the Pedometer to prove who was right. It was an exciting change from the guns, knives, and other instruments of violence which comprised the offers of most radio shows of the thirties. It was, of course, possible to buy a professional Boy Scout Pedometer at your neighborhood scouting supplies store, but that would cost a few dollars. Jack's came to you practically free for a boxtop from Wheaties and 10¢ in coin. The Pedometer offers started in 1936, and proved popular with two generations of radio fans. Today, it would cost you from $10 to $20 to lay your hands on one of those original hike-recorders. Jack frequently used the instrument to chart the correct course out of unspeakable horrors that lay in wait for him on his (almost) never ceasing quest for adventure—and audience.

Terry and the Pirates

Terry and the Pirates had two separate shots as a radio series. The first ran from 1937 to 1939, and the second, for Quaker Oats, from 1943 to 1948. The radio version was rather faithful to Milt Caniff's comic strip, and included Hotshot Charlie, Flip Corcoran, Pat Ryan, and, of course, the Dragon Lady.

After World War Two ended, people did not seem to wish to be reminded of the event, so the show's popularity fell off sharply. A television version appeared in 1953, but the venture (sponsored on alternate Saturdays by Canada Dry ginger ale) was not a huge success.

The premium from *Terry* most sought after by collectors is the Gold Detector Ring of 1947. A look through the telescope-like device mounted on the ring's band gave you a magnified view of a piece of real gold ore. That way, those of you who decide to hunt for a gold mine will know what to look for, and will recognize gold when you've found it. That ring is worth up to $35 today.

A record pressed in 1948 with an illustration of Terry on the label is currently valued at about $20.

Flash Gordon

Although Flash Gordon made it big as a televison serial, he never did make a very big impact in the premium giveaway field. Created by Alex Raymond in the 1930's, Flash was featured in the funnies, in comic books, and, finally, on radio and television. There is a space

The Terry and the Pirates Gold Detector Ring (1947) gives you a peek at the real thing!

This movable-arm decoder lets you send secret messages and decipher the ones sent to you.

This Dick Tracy Detective Club Shield Badge dates from about 1937.

This Secret Service Pinback Membership Button, one of many Dick Tracy premiums offered in 1938, is a good buy at about $6.

The Dick Tracy Air Detective Pin (1938) typifies the character's involvement with flying.

compass bearing this hero's name, and it is worth about $25 today. A 1948 phonograph record (78's anyone?) and a two-way telephone each carry about the same current value in the marketplace.

Dick Tracy

Dick Tracy was another show of comic book origin that had a difficult time transferring to radio. At least, Tracy had a tough time holding down a steady sponsor and time slot. He hopped around between NBC and Mutual from 1935 until he was finally cancelled in 1939. He then returned to the air in 1943 and managed to survive until 1948. All this hopping around makes it extremely difficult to date many of his premiums with any degree of reliability. There were, however, many pieces of equipment for junior G-Men.

One beaut was a gigantic pencil that wrote in red from one end and in blue from the other. The cap had a whistle that sounded like a siren when you blew through it. It must have been great to stop traffic, so you could use the pencil to write out a summons. That pencil brings up to $25 today.

There were, of course, lots of badges which were available for a number of Quaker Oats seals—and a whole slew of aviator equipment. Tracy, at one time, was into flying even more wholeheartedly than Captain Midnight.

The Dick Tracy Wrist Watch was first produced by the New Haven Watch Company around 1934, and sold then for $2.65. If you are really lucky, you might be able to get one of those today for between $125 and $150. Later models of his watch are commanding only slightly less.

A toy put out by the Marx Company, the Dick Tracy Official Squad Car, a friction powered piece of tin, is now worth about $20, and all sorts of other gadgets associated with the character have climbed to rather formidable price levels. Pocket knives, whistles, and secret compartment rings are but a few of the items that were offered as premiums or over-the-counter—and their prices seem destined to go no way but up.

The Dick Tracy Hat Ring is enamelled. A 1936 or '37 premium, it is worth about $20.

Space Patrol

Ed Kemmer has appeared on television soap operas and on an occasional TV commercial, but in the heart of every adult who was a child in the 1950's, he will be remembered as Commander Buzz Corey of the Spa-a-a-ace Patro-o-o-l. Commander Corey's first mission for the United Planets was heard in 1950 over the ABC radio network. Eventually, under the sponsorship of Wheat Chex and Rice Chex (remember Ralston's?), the programs were simulcast over ABC-TV. Major Roberts was played by Jack Narz, who has since gained recognition as a perennial host of daytime game shows. Cadet Happy provided the laughs.

Doctor Scarno and Prince Bacharatti were the evil scientific masterminds that most frequently surfaced in pursuit of their modest ambi-

The plastic Space Patrol Membership Pin was a Ralston premium circa 1951. It's valued today at about $20.

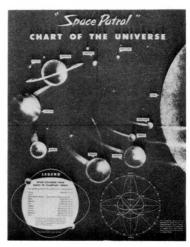

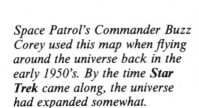

*Space Patrol's Commander Buzz Corey used this map when flying around the universe back in the early 1950's. By the time **Star Trek** came along, the universe had expanded somewhat.*

tion—domination of the universe—and the headquarters of the Space Patrol was Terra, a man-made planet slightly larger than Earth.

The premiums offered by Buzz were not exactly phenomenal, nor were they extensive, but they have increased steadily in value over the years, so that they range up to $50 or $55 in value. The Decoder Belt and Buckle and the Rocket Ring are the two most sought after premiums from this show.

The discovery of "Planet X" was a pivotal point in the show's run, and several premiums were generated from that episode. There was even a "Name that Planet Contest." A "Name that Planet Contest" letter is worth up to $15 today.

Despite the fact that the show lasted for only five years, it must be remembered that for four of those years it was sponsored by the greatest premium believer in the universe: The Ralston Company.

Though worlds apart, The Lone Ranger and Tom Corbett, Space Cadet, may still come together . . . wherever collectors gather.

CHAPTER VI

A Price Guide to Premiums

The premiums listed in this chapter are listed with prices for specimens in *good* condition and in *mint* condition. "Mint" means just that—appearing as if they had never even been handled. "Good" means that all parts and/or pages are present, but that there may be some creases, chipped paint, or other damage that make the item not as valuable as a new one. "Fine" condition is somewhere in between mint and good. An item in fine condition will be worth an amount between the mint and good prices depending on how much the condition of the item approaches one or the other. For that reason, we have shown no price for fine. Objects in "poor" condition are obviously worse than good. They may have parts missing, and may, in fact, not be worth having at all. A rule of thumb worth following is not to pay any more for an item than it is worth to you.

Generally speaking, whether you are a buyer or a seller, and interested in collecting as a hobby or as an investment, you should be aware that now—and probably for all time—it will be the items selling for between $10 and $30 that will very likely never go begging. Higher priced objects will not evoke nearly as much interest when offered for sale, because there simply are not that many people willing or able to spend hundreds of dollars on collectibles.

At this time, radio premiums are turning up by the carload at antique shows and stores, flea markets, and estate sales. Old attics are yielding treasure troves as estate dealers buy whole houses of furniture for the "true antiques," and routinely ship out cartons filled with nostalgia to dealers and mail order houses. Nostalgia items—especially those associated with radio and/or comic book characters are good investments, but don't get carried away. There are never any guarantees, and that is a fact of life that everybody would do well to remember.

Amos 'n' Andy

	Good	Mint
Stand-Up Cardboard Figures (1930)	$ 30	$ 75
Puzzle	5	20
Map of Weber City (including envelope and letter) (1935)	12	25
Sheet Music for "The Perfect Song"	1	5

Bobby Benson

H-O Ranger Club Button (1932)	2	7
Photos (set of 6) of Bobby and the gang	6	14
Code Book (1935)	10	12
Tunnel of Gold book	10	20
The Lost Herd book	10	20

Buck Rogers in the 25th Century

From Kellogg's (1932–33)

Buck Rogers' origin (storybook)	40	80

From Cocomalt (1933–35)

Solar Map	100	200
Buck and Wilma picture	18	30
4-color Adventure Book Offer Sheet	12	40
Cut-Out Adventure Book (intact)	150	230
City of Floating Globes book (1935)	25	50

From Cream of Wheat (1935–36)

Solar Scout Manual	35	80
Solar Scout Badge	18	40
Flight Commander Whistle Badge	25	50
Chief Explorer Badge	25	50
Solar Scout Sweater Emblem	20	50
Solar Scout Knife	32	80
Wilma Pendant Medallion	20	50
Repeller Ray Seal Ring	60	110

Solar Scouts and other youngsters who didn't like Cream of Wheat made a point of seeing that their parents knew about the latest "genuine official Buck Rogers 25th Century equipment" when holiday time rolled around.

The following are store items that were redeemable for Green Triangles obtainable by eating your Cream of Wheat:

	Good	Mint
Disintegrator Pistol with Holster	30	80
Balsa Spaceship Model	5	15
Lead Figures of *Buck Rogers* Characters (each)	9	20
School Bag	6	17
Interplanetary Game	35	100
Red Pencil Box	5	12
Movie Projector	20	35
Films for Movie Projector	4	10
Rubber Stamp Set	20	45
Lite-Blaster Flashlight	10	30
Uniform	25	80
Helmet	12	35

1939–52

	Good	Mint
Popsicle Pete Radio News Premium Catalog	9	20
Dog Tag (1942, 1943)	12	27
Blue Green Glo-in-Dark Crocodile Ring (red stone)	20	50
Initial Ring (with birthstone)	30	60
Charm Bracelet	30	75
Sylvania Space Rangers Kit (1952)	12	35

Buster Brown Gang
(later Smilin' Ed's Gang)

	Good	Mint
Bandana (1946)	6	16
Buster Brown Ring (with Squeeky the Mouse and Froggy the Gremlin)	10	20
Buster Brown Comics #1 (1945)	6	12

Captain Midnight

Skelly Premiums (1939)

	Good	Mint
Photo of Captain Midnight wearing Secret Ring	12	20
Photo of Chuck or of Patsy	7	10

	Good	Mint
Photo of the Gang	10	15
Trick and Riddle Book	10	20
Mysto-Magic Weather Forecasting Flight Wings	4	7
Skelly Premiums (1940–41)		
Flight Patrol Membership Medal	5	10
Jumping Bean Game	15	25
American Airline Map	35	80
Flight Patrol Newspaper		
Vol. 1, No. 1	18	45
Vol. 1, No. 2	10	32
Ovaltine Premiums (1940–41)		
Secret Squadron Manual	35	65
Mystery Dial Code-O-Graph	15	25
Flight Commander Ring	10	18
Detect-O-Scope	25	60
Whistling Whirlwind Ring	25	50
Pilot's Badge	10	20
Torpedo Bombers	20	40
1942		
Secret Squadron Manual	22	45
Photomatic Code-O-Graph Badge		
with Captain Midnight's picture	25	40
without Captain Midnight's picture	10	20
Flight Commander Flying Cross	35	80
Flight Commander Handbook	20	30
Sliding Secret Compartment Ring	25	50
Mystic Eye Detector Ring	18	25
Shake-Up Mug	12	25
Plane Detector	20	40
Mystic Dog Whistle	15	25
1943		
Shoulder Patch	10	25
Folder with Insignia	10	20
1944		
Service Ribbon	20	40
Shoulder Patch	10	30

1945	Good	Mint
Secret Squadron Manual	25	50
Magni-Magic Code-O-Graph Badge	20	30
Mystic Sun-God Ring	35	75

1946		
Secret Squadron Official Manual	25	45
Mirro-Flash Code-O-Graph Badge	12	25

1947		
Secret Squadron Manual	20	40
Whistling Code-O-Graph	15	25
Printing Signet Ring	30	45

1948		
Manual	20	40
Mirro-Matic Code-O-Graph	15	25
Spy Scope	10	20

1949		
Secret Squadron Code and Manual	20	40
Key-O-Matic Code-O-Graph Decoder	12	23
Insignia Transfer Decals	7	18

1955–56

It is difficult to differentiate which premiums were offered which year, but the SS designation was changed during this time to SQ. Can you guess why?

	Good	Mint
Secret Squadron Manual	15	25
Membership Card	15	25
Photo Decal of Captain Midnight	4	6
Flight Commander Commission	10	17
SQ Patch	10	20

1957		
Secret Squadron Manual	14	25
Membership Card	5	10
Flight Commander Plastic Signet Ring	15	30
15th Anniversary Shake-Up Mug	10	20
Hot Ovaltine Mug	5	15
SQ 15th Anniversary Cloth Patch	10	20

Chandu the Magician

	Good	Mint
Chinese Coin Trick	20	35
Buddha Money Mystery	25	50
Holiday Trick	20	30
Svengali Mind Reading Trick	30	50
Galloping Coin Trick	30	50
Choco-mint Mystery	30	50

Cisco Kid

	Good	Mint
Secret Compartment Picture Ring	20	30
Triple S Club Kit (1951)	25	50
Face Mask of the Cisco Kid or of Pancho (1953) (each)	5	15

Counterspy

1949

	Good	Mint
Counterspy Agent Photo Badge	15	25
Membership Certificate	10	18

Dick Tracy

Pre-1938

	Good	Mint
Detective Club Shield Badge	10	25
Hat Ring (enamelled)	20	25

1938

	Good	Mint
Secret Code Book	20	40
Pinback Membership Button	5	10
Sergeant's Badge	13	20
Lieutenant's Badge	15	30
Captain's Badge	22	45
Inspector General's Badge	30	50
Secret Service Patrol Badge, Girl's Division	10	20

	Good	Mint
Lucky Bangle Bracelet	15	40
Secret Detecto Kit	20	35
Siren Plane	35	45
Air Detective Cap	17	28
Air Detective Pin	15	23
Air Detective Ring	22	40
Wing Bracelet	30	50
Ring (secret compartment)	35	50

1939

	Good	Mint
Methods and Magic Tricks Manual	12	25
Pocket Flashlight	15	25
Siren Pencil	17	28
Telephones	30	40
Flagship Rocket Plane	35	60
Complete Detective Kit	40	60

Don Winslow of the Navy

The Don Winslow adventure series began in 1937 and lasted about as long as World War Two. They were sponsored first by Kellogg's and later by Post Toasties. They favored peace rather than war.

1938

	Good	Mint
Good Luck Coin	10	20

1939

	Good	Mint
Creed and Manual of the Squadron of Peace	25	50
Ensign Pin	15	30

This Lieutenant Commander Pin was offered by Don Winslow of the Navy in 1939 for somewhat less than the $40 it can bring today from a collector.

	Good	Mint
Lieutenant Commander Pin	20	40
Serial Number Member's Ring	35	50
Periscope	10	30

1940

	Good	Mint
Photo of Don and Red Pennington	6	15
Code Sheet	15	25

Frank Buck (Bring 'em Back Alive)

Frank Buck's exploits, as an animal trainer who bagged the animals himself, was widely publicized by circus promoters of the thirties. The show fizzled, but had a brief comeback in the forties.

1934

	Good	Mint
Adventure Club Handbook	20	40
Adventure Club Pinback Button	5	13

1939

	Good	Mint
Genuine Ivory Initial Ring	22	45
Ivory Knife	15	28
Explorers Club Leopard Ring	35	75
Explorers Sun Dial Watch (1949)	12	25

Frank Buck would never have been able to "bring 'em back alive" in 1939 without his autographed, ivory-handled knife.

When Frank Buck was on safari in the jungle, he used his Sun Dial Watch (1949) to tell when it was time to make camp for the night.

Gabby Hayes	Good	Mint
Shooting Cannon Ring (1951)	22	35

Green Hornet

	Good	Mint
Secret Compartment Glow-in-the-Dark Seal Ring (1947)	75	120

Jack Armstrong—The All American Boy

1933

	Good	Mint
Big Ten Football Game	20	40
Daisy Shooting Propeller Plane Gun	25	60

1934

Hand Exerciser	8	13
Hike-O-Meter (red)	15	30
Photo of Jack and the Gang	5	15

1935

Secret Bombsight (with 3 bombs)	60	100

1936

Dragon Talisman Map with Spinner and Brass Talisman	50	100
Hike-O-Meter (blue)	10	20
Belt Flashlight	10	18

1937

Telescope	10	20
Sound Effects Kit	15	40

1938

Magic Answer Box	20	40
Egyptian Whistle Ring	20	30
Bullet Flashlights (each of red, blue, and black)	12	20

1939

Magnetic Key	20	40
Catapult Plane	30	40
Cereal Bowl	4	10

	Good	Mint
1940		
Dragon's Eye Ring	20	35
Luminous Gardenia Bracelet	20	35
Airplane	20	30
1941		
Pedometer (aluminum rim)	10	25
1942		
Write a Fighter Corps Manual	22	45
1943		
Future Champions Cloth Patch	10	20
1944		
Model Airplanes:		
Curtiss P-40 and Japanese Zero set	10	20
Spitfire V and Focke-Wulf 190 set	10	20
Fairey Fulmar and Heinkel 113 set	10	20
P-47 Thunderbolt and Yak 26 set	10	20
P-39 Airacobra and Russian IL-2 set	10	20
P-51 Mustang and Aichi Dive Bomber set	10	20
1945		
Complete Pre-Flight Training Kit	45	75
Pre-Flight Trainer Model	15	22
World War II airplanes re-offered on Wheaties packages (set of 10)	30	50

Lone Ranger

	Good	Mint
1935		
Photo of the Lone Ranger (black and white)	5	10
Silvercup Safety Scout Badge	7	14
Chief Scout Badge	28	50
1936		
Miami Maid Membership Badge	8	15
1938–40		
Four-color photo	5	10
Good Luck Token	5	10

	Good	Mint
Safety Club Membership Stars from Bond Bread,		
Butternut Bread, Eddy's, and QBC Bread	7	14
Safety Club News:		
Vol. 1, No. 1 (1939)	10	17
Vol. 1, No. 2–No. 6 (each)	7	10
Solid Silver Bullet	5	8

1941

	Good	Mint
National Defenders Secret Portfolio	12	30
National Defenders Warning Siren	15	30
Glow-in-the-Dark Safety Belt	20	50
Secret Compartment Silver Bullet (with silver ore		
inside)	15	25
Tooled Leather Texas Cattleman's Belt	15	25
Hi-Yo Silver Polo Shirt	13	20

1942

	Good	Mint
Secret Compartment Ring (with Army, Navy, Air		
Force, or Marine insignia on sliding panel)	30	50
Victory Corps Manual	20	40
Victory Corps Tab	20	28

1943

	Good	Mint
Blackout Kit	10	20
Pedometer	10	20
Compass Silver Bullet	13	25

1947

	Good	Mint
Atom Bomb Ring	12	25
Weather Ring	18	25
Flashlight Gun (with secret compartment handle)	20	30

1948

	Good	Mint
Frontier Town (all 4 sections)	75	200
Flashlight Ring	20	30
Six-Shooter Ring (with real sparks!)	15	30

1949

	Good	Mint
Marine Corps Scenes Movie Ring	20	35

1951

	Good	Mint
Secret Compartment Deputy's Badge	10	19

Radio Orphan Annie

	Good	Mint
Photo of Little Orphan Annie	8	15
"Little Orphan Annie's Song" Sheet Music	5	9
Photo of Annie and Joe Buttons	10	15
Shake-Up Game	5	12

1932
	Good	Mint
Annie Mug (ceramic)	12	22
Shake-Up Mug—Type I	12	19

1933
	Good	Mint
Orphan Annie Mask	20	29
Treasure Hunt Game	15	30

1934
	Good	Mint
Manual	20	27
Secret Society Pin (bronze)	7	10
Silver Star Pin	10	15
Silver Star Manual	12	19
Orphan Annie Face Ring	12	18
Wonder Robot Book	20	32
Identification Bracelet	20	30

1935
	Good	Mint
Manual	20	30
Round Decoder Pin	15	21

1936
	Good	Mint
Manual	15	23
Secret Compartment Decoder Pin	12	17
Silver Star Ring (crossed keys on star—Secret Society)	20	30
Map of Simmons Corners	30	45

1937
	Good	Mint
Manual	20	27
Sunburst Decoder Pin	14	19
Silver Star Secret Message Ring	20	35
Shake-Up Mug	15	25
Talking Stationery Set	20	35

	Good	Mint
School Pin	10	15
Two-Initial Signet Ring	15	23

1938

	Good	Mint
Manual	20	29
Telematic Decoder Pin	15	20
Silver Star Triple Mystery Secret Compartment Ring	30	40
Silver Star Manual	15	20
Shake-Up Mug (green)	15	35
Sun Watch	15	23

1939

	Good	Mint
Manual	26	36
Mysto-Matic Decoder	12	16
Identification Tag Bracelet	20	30
Mystic Eye Look-Around Ring	25	37

1940

	Good	Mint
Manual	25	35
Code Captain Belt and Buckle	25	45
Shake-Up Mug	15	25
Dog Whistle	15	25

1941

	Good	Mint
Secret Guard Handbook	25	35
Mysto-Snapper Membership Badge (clicker)	7	13
Secret Guard Initial Ring	20	30
Secret Guard Magnifying Ring	30	40
Secret Guard Insignia Cap	15	23
Secret Guard Penlight	15	25
Secret Guard Detecto-Kit	15	26

1942

	Good	Mint
Secret Guard Handbook	25	35
Whirl-O-Matic Decoder (cardboard)	25	31
Whistle Badge	11	19

Roy Rogers

	Good	Mint
Secret Code Manual	25	32
Sterling Silver Hat Ring (signed across the brim)	15	21

Radio Orphan Annie's 1938 Telematic Decoder Pin was "the most important secret symbol of Radio Orphan Annie's Secret Society!"

	Good	Mint
1948		
Branding Iron Ring	23	30
1949		
Microscope Ring	20	27
1950		
Deputy Star Badge (secret compartment and whistle on back)	12	20
Plastic Toby Mug of Roy	5	7

Sergeant Preston of the Yukon

	Good	Mint
1949		
Pedometer	15	20
Signal Flashlight	25	35
Yukon Trail (59 cardboard models from Quaker Puffed Wheat and Rice boxes)	60	160
Mounted Police Whistle	10	15
Totem Pole Collection (set includes Thunderbird, Fight with Otters, Burial Pole, Killer Whale, and Sun and Raven)	30	60
Dog Cards (set of 35, each)	.25	.55
Skinning Knife	15	20
Gold Ore Detector	35	55
1955		
Yukon Square-Inch Land Deed	13	17
Map of Yukon Territory	17	29
1956		
Membership Button	20	40
Ten-in-One Trail Kit	25	45
Comic Books (pocket size)		
How He Became a Mountie	5	7
How Yukon King Saved Him from the Wolves	5	7
How He Became a Sergeant	5	7

The Shadow

	Good	Mint
Shadow Photo	20	35
Shadow Club Stud Pin (pulp premium)	85	120
Blue Coal (glow-in-the-dark plastic) Ring	80	170
Blue Coal Ink Blotter (four-color)	8	15
Blue Coal Match Book	15	30
Crocodile Ring with black stone (Carey Salt—1947)	35	75

Sky King

Tele Blinker Ring	40	60
Navajo Treasure Ring (1950)	35	45
Spy-Detecto Writer	35	50
Electronic Television Ring (1949)	25	45
Magni-Glo Writing Ring (1949)	20	30
Radar Signal Ring	35	65
Mystery Picture Ring	30	40
Detecto Microscope	40	50
Aztec Indian Ring	35	45
Secret Signalscope (1947)	30	42

Space Patrol

1951–54

Membership Pin (plastic)	14	25
Chart of the Universe	30	40
Cosmic Smoke Gun (1952)	25	35
Walkie Talkies, pair	20	30
Premium Folders	15	20
Interplanetary Stamp Album and Stamps	15	27
Periscope	30	40
Decoder Buckle and Belt	35	55
Cap	20	30
Rocket Flashlight	25	35
Rocket Ring	40	60

Superman, The Adventures of

	Good	Mint
Crusaders Ring	40	70
Walkie Talkie (1945)	16	24
Pep Silver Metal Airplane Ring (1948)	20	25
F-87 "Super Jet" Black Plastic Airplane Ring (1948)	20	35

Superman–Tim Premiums

Membership Button (profile)	15	25
Membership Button (Tim's head in circle)	15	25
Membership Card	8	15
Tim Club Ring	25	52
Monthly Manuals (1942)	11	29
Superman Good Stuff Sweatshirt	20	35
Superman Red Backs	3	6

Tarzan

Radio Club Badge:		
Drink More Milk	25	55
Bursley Coffees	35	65
Radio Club Girl's Bracelet (1934)	40	70
Statues (Fould's noodle products)		
Tarzan	15	23
Jane Porter	10	14
Witch Doctor	10	17
Three Monkeys set	7	9
Cannibal	10	17
Water Color Set	12	24

Terry and the Pirates

Gold Detector Ring (1947)	25	35
Comic Strip Cast Drawings (set of 5)	30	40

Tom Mix

	Good	Mint
1933		
Life of Tom Mix Manual (with Horseshoe Nail Ring instructions)	25	45
Life of Tom Mix Manual and Premium Catalog (enlarged edition)	33	50
Straight Shooters Cloth Emblem	25	40
Bandana	25	40
Wooden Gun (opens and cylinder spins, rubber markings from stamp on handle)	40	70
Genuine Leather Cuffs	30	40
Spinning Rope	30	37
Cowboy Hat	35	55
Spurs with Leather TM Strap	40	50
1934		
Lariat Tricks and Stunts Booklet	23	35
Premium Catalog	15	25
1935		
Straight Shooters Ring	25	35
Branding Iron	30	40
Leather Cuffs with TM Bar Brand	30	40
Wooden Gun in Holster and Cartridge Belt	60	115
Straight Shooter Stationery	15	25
Western Movie (cardboard with 30-frame paper movie)	35	55
Leather Strap Lucky Wrist Band	25	35
Sun Watch	30	39
1936		
Wooden Gun (revolving cylinder, does not open, cardboard handle)	40	70
Rocket Parachute	35	60
Premium Catalog	15	25
Championship Belt (red & black checkerboard) and Buckle	30	50
Buckle only	19	28

	Good	Mint
1937		
Compass Magnifying Glass	12	25
Signet (initial) Ring	35	50
Postal Telegraph Set (blue)	27	48
Gold Straight Shooters Badge	20	35
Silver Straight Shooters Badge	22	45
Movie Make-Up Kit (first version)	30	45
1938		
Telescope	25	40
Photo in Silver Frame	32	47
Telephone Set	35	50
Ranch Boss Badge	35	55
Mystery Look-In Picture Ring (recently found in quantity)	20	27
Bullet Flashlight (nickel plated brass with paper decal)	27	40
1939		
Periscope	45	65
Pen and Pencil Set	15	27
Wooden Gun (no moving parts)	30	50
Pocket Knife	27	37
1940		
Gold Ore Charm	25	35
Gold Ore Assayer's Certificate	15	25
Brass Compass and Magnifier	28	43
Electric Telegraph Signal Set	25	40
1941		
Six Gun Decoder Badge	20	35
Manual (16 pages)	30	40
1942		
Signature Ring	25	37
1944		
Secret Manual	33	50
Spinning Siren Ring	30	40
Magnet Ring	23	35

	Good	Mint
1945		
Glow-in-Dark Ribbon and Medal	35	55
Story Manual (with chuck wagon on front, original)	25	35
1946		
Look Around Ring	27	40
Glow-in-the-Dark Compass Magnifying Glass	17	27
Curley Bradley Fan Post Card	12	20
Pinback Decoder Buttons Set	15	30
1947		
Identification Bracelet	19	29
1948		
Rocket Parachute	50	70
Mystery of the Flaming Warrior Book (in dust jacket)	30	55
Gun and Arrowhead Compass	31	45
1949		
Glow-in-the-Dark Spurs (aluminum with glo rowels)	25	35
Sliding Whistle Ring	27	39
Lucite Signal Arrowhead	20	30
1950		
Magic-Light Tiger-Eye Ring (plastic)	40	60
Golden Plastic Bullet Telescope with Magic Tone Birdcall	15	25

CHAPTER VII

Looking Toward the Future

If you are looking at memorabilia collecting with an eye toward the future, there are two directions in which to look: the past, and the present. The premiums which have already been discussed or mentioned in the foregoing pages are still (for the most part) good investments. They are not likely to decrease in value, for with the exception of those few items where stores have recently come to light, the supply is not expected to increase dramatically but rather decrease—and the demand *is* increasing, quite rapidly in fact, as more and more people are being bitten by the collecting bug.

Those items which you can obtain for ten dollars or less today are likely to be in the ten to twenty dollar range within a year or two, and so should be considered worthwhile investments, if you are interested in mere monetary appreciation. By and large, however, collectors are going into memorabilia for reasons quite different from financial considerations. Some are out to procure and hold onto small pieces of Americana: pieces which have an intrinsic worth to them as part of their own personal history; pieces to be passed on to future generations of children and grandchildren with a message. That message might be: "Hey, here is what things were like when I was growing up." Perhaps, they just feel good holding onto pieces of their past, or maybe they rather fancy the appearance of something that they saw at a dealer's or at a flea market, and want to have it for their very own.

In short, there are nearly as many reasons for collecting memorabilia as there are collectors—which means that every day there are more and more reasons. Some people collect only items associated with a single character. Others collect anything they can get their hands on. Still others are interested in products offered by a single company, items made of a certain material (metal, paper, glo-plastic), or items with a single purpose (watches, war toys, decoders, etc.).

Premiums are not being offered today at the same pace at which they were in the thirties, forties or fifties, yet there are still enough things around that can be sent away for. Today, you will generally have to send from 50¢ to a dollar along with your boxtops, and yet the plastic items that will arrive still have an appeal all their own—especially if you still are a kid at heart.

Actually, being a kid at heart probably has a great deal to do with the increase in value of memorabilia—being a kid and wanting to remain so, at least in some small (or large) corner of your life. Childhood is the time that most of us associate with "fun," and wishing to hold on to that fun feeling is not a desire to be taken too lightly in these complex times.

Things sold over the counter are often as good as premiums—many times even better—if you are trying to store things away for twenty years or so hence. Speculation can be aided by a look at which items from twenty years ago are demanding such high prices today. First of

Lots of kids had fun in the fifties when it was Howdy Doody time. Ovaltine joined in by offering a Howdy Doody Mug to drink (blank) out of.

all, almost all of the collectibles that we have dealt with have been associated with characters—and goodness knows, there is no shortage of characters right now. Many of the old ones (Batman, Superman, Wonder Woman) are still with us, while others are constantly being created. The Hulk, Captain America, and other figures of the Marvel Comics Group will probably be recognized on for-sale items at flea markets and antique shows in the year 2010. So will television figures such as the captain and crew of the Federation Starship *Enterprise:* Captain Kirk, Mr. Spock, Dr. McCoy, etc. The motion picture *Star Wars* seems to be gathering to itself (and to sequels?) a cult following and Luke Skywalker, R2D2, and C3PO, Darth Vader, Princess Leia, Obi Wan Kenobi and Han Solo may be in considerable demand by the turn of the century. Don't forget your friendly neighborhood Spiderman, either.

Remember, too, that it is those figures who are really important to children during their growing-up years that will again become important to them as collecting adults. Who could be more important in the 1990's to the children of the seventies than Bert and Ernie, Kermit the Frog, Big Bird, Grover, or the Cookie Monster?

Although we have mentioned several times in earlier chapters the value that has accrued to paper collectibles, such as figures clipped from cereal boxes and yearly radio-show manuals, a stroll through any antique show or flea market will show you that metal items are very much in vogue. I don't mean just precious metals (when are *they* not in demand?), but metals used for things like cigarette boxes, packaging from various candies and throat lozenges, and figurines—to cite but a few examples. It is a good deal easier to collect and preserve metal objects than paper ones, for obvious reasons, and there is every reason to believe that fine examples of metal craftsmanship and artistry will continue to command attention thirty years hence.

The foregoing notwithstanding, let us face up to the fact that the material most representative of our age is plastic. Everything from model automobiles to full-size jumbo jets are available with a large percentage of plastic parts. If the craftsmen of the Ming Dynasty were plying their vase-making vocation today, who is to say how much of their art might not be in lucite and acrylics. The message, then, is do not shun potential collectibles because of the material that they are made of. The very fact that *Star Trek* figures come in bendable plastic makes them representative of 1970's and 1980's Americana. Collectors of the next century would no more accept a stuffed cloth Captain Kirk than they would a plastic Raggedy Ann.

Ample space has been devoted in these pages to a discussion of where to find collectibles of the past. It is only fitting, therefore, that we examine the subject of where to look for collectibles of the present. Probably the first place to look is the last place that might occur to you—your own home.

What do you have lying around the house right now that is likely to be in demand by collectors thirty years from now? Some of the answers might shock you. Have you had a can of beer lately? Beer can collectors are becoming legion in this country. A volume entitled *The Beer Can Collector's Bible* has sold more than twenty thousand copies in hardcover alone. Perhaps when you finish your next brew you should wash the can out and store it in tissue paper. When did you last see a Coca Cola bottle with a pry-off cork-lined lid? *There's* a collector's item for you. Do you have a book of Triple-S Blue Stamps or one partially filled with King Korn Stamps? The list is virtually endless.

What is sitting in the bottom of a drawer or on the back of a closet shelf that is likely to be tossed away at the next Spring Cleanup? Are there any photographs of the Beatles? They don't pose anymore, you know. Have you a promotional photo manual that sold for $2 at the movie theater when you saw *Star Wars* for the first time? What about the McDonald's tumbler that you were warned not to let your kids drink from because the paint contained lead? How many people do you think held onto those?

The key phrase, in deciding what holds potential for the future as a collectible that will increase in value, is "common sense." If a fad lasts a few short months and then is gone from the scene without leaving more than a ten word imprint upon your personal memorybank, it will certainly not conjure up any great feelings of nostalgia in future generations. Do you remember a motion picture called "The Day the Earth Stood Still?" It was a good movie. It contained a robot that could melt tanks with one glance. There was also a rather impressive alien in the guise of Michael Rennie. All talk of the movie was over three months later. No C3PO or Chewbacca, they. Zorro never captured the imagination the way that other masked man did. And do you remember Moonbase Alpha? Well, in case you do not, it has been only a year since *Space: 1999* went off the air. Do you know how long it has been since *Star Trek* completed its first run?

A good rule of thumb to follow is to ask yourself whether a certain character has made a lasting impression upon the members of your family. Will Fonzie endure long after *Happy Days* turn sad? There are Fonzie dolls and Fonzie posters, and . . . Well you just look in the store and see what else. Now Barbie and Ken—they never even had a program of their own, but I'm willing to predict that their future place will be secure long after Donny and Marie have had their teeth capped.

Probably most people are unaware that the longest running television shows of this era are the soap operas. Millions of people—men and women alike—tune in afternoon after afternoon to see how Doctor Bill will handle the case of Julia McInnes who is dying of the rare but incurable disease, Jurgens Myesthenia, an illness in which your nose slides right off your face. Meanwhile, Julia's husband, Andrew, is playing around with his wife's nurse during visiting hours in the used-linens closet. Is Samantha really pregnant? If she is, is it George's baby or Kurt's? Is Kurt really pregnant, or is he just trying to get Darlene's sympathy? And what about Cecilia?

Despite the fascination that the soaps obviously hold for their daily audience, and despite their obvious durability, they do not spawn collectibles. Moreover, the *"As the World Turns* Game" is not likely to be a sought after premium thirty years hence. Actually, the character of collectibles from the shows of the sixties and seventies are quite different from those of the thirties, forties, and fifties. Premiums of the type that were offered in radio's heyday simply are not offered today. That was a simpler time, and the techniques of marketing and packaging programs, characters, and products were still being explored. The audience, too, was far less sophisticated—although you might not know it, looking at much of the trash that passes for entertainment now. The craftsmanship and artistry that went into the free premiums of the golden age of radio cannot be recaptured at the current rates of pay for artisans if the company still hopes to turn a profit. Remember, wages were lower, and jobs—especially during the Depression—were scarce. Why not manufacture a decoder—or two? Or a ring, badge, kit, or shake-up mug for that matter.

Nowadays, the collectibles being marketed take the form of commercially distributed products. The common denominator, though, remains the same. The item should be identified inseparably with a popular character or show, and should excite the imagination of its owner. Beyond those requirements, the rest is speculation. It is easy to predict that *Star Trek* memorabilia will some day be worth money. A set of *Star Trek* communicators that operate on the Citizens' Band are exciting to any child, and will hold memories for that child when he/she is an adult. On the other hand, Starbuck and the Cylons of *Battlestar Galactica* will probably not make a lasting impression, although there certainly is enough paraphernalia being disseminated by the toy manufacturers in connection with this series. However, that was also true of *Space: 1999*—already a proven dud!

Wrist watches associated with characters and shows are also good bets. *Star Wars, Star Trek, Spiderman,* and so on, have been immortalized beneath plastic crystals. Each tick denotes a timeless quality, real or aspired to. No longer are watches available for the $1.89 that at one time might have gotten you Dick Tracy's face on a timepiece, yet if they appreciate at the same rate in thirty years that Tracy watches have (10,000 percent), they are well worth the $16.99 or so that they currently cost.

What is worth collecting? We have offered many guidelines, but in the final analysis you must be the judge. Mickey Mouse and Bugs Bunny are timeless, but because of their timelessness, the only items associated with them that are likely to increase in value are those spawned during their childhood (baby-mouse and bunnyhood?). They represent the opposite end of the spectrum to *Space: 1999*. Their timelessness has glutted the market with specimens that immortalize their images. Virtually no home in this country is without a likeness of one or the other—at least no home that houses a child.

You might almost say that the wheel has come full circle. Many of the radio characters that provided the premiums of the thirties, forties, and fifties had their birth in the funny pages—as they once were called. These characters became the folk heroes of America for three generations or more. It was in their names and bearing their images, drawn by some of the finest graphic artists that this country or any other has ever produced, that hundreds of premiums were produced to give substance to our and our parents' imaginations. Now, while a few television shows and motion pictures have had the ability to foment the rising of cults of admirers, adherents, and adorers, it is once more from the comic books—today's "funny pages"—that today's superheroes are emerging. Our childrens' allegiances go to Captain America, Thor, the Hulk, the Avengers, the members of the Justice League (including Superman, Batman, and Wonder Woman), the Green Lantern, the

Silver Surfer, and the like. Each time a new character is born in the comics, the issue in which he or she has been created becomes an instant collector's item. It is also, in all likelihood, the images and equipment bearing the mark of these superheroes that will command the attention of collectors thirty years hence.

Still, there are many collectibles from the thirties, and especially from the forties and fifties, still showing up today, as estates are sold, and trunks are taken out of long ignored attics. You can speculate upon what may be big in the future, or you can go for those memorabilia which are now proving their merit by virtue of their being able to attract a following. If you decide to go this route, you should find this book a most valuable guide.

Remember, too, do not look for expensive items if you are seeking to invest, because they are the ones that are least likely to be in demand later on. The greatest demand is for goods in the under $30 price range. Of course, the more under $30 you go, the greater the demand is. Only a really avid collector with a pretty hefty bankroll is about to buy a $150 character wrist watch. Original Mickey Mouse timepieces, incidentally, have brought $500 or more. Remember, though, for anything that you have to sell, the estimated worth is irrelevant if there is not a potential buyer willing to pay that price.

The world of collecting lies open, just waiting for new adherents to pass through its portal. Do not enter, however, if your main concern is future financial gain. By the time you accrue your fortune through memorabilia—if you, in fact, ever do—you will probably be too old to enjoy the fruits of the financial gains that you've made. You might not even be around at all!

Enter the world of collecting for the pleasure that owning beautiful, rare, nostalgic, or novelty items will give to you in the here and now and over the years to come. Memorabilia collecting is to the middle class person what collecting old masters is to the wealthy. It is an opportunity to appreciate owning works of art. Possible future gains are only hoped for. Never, but *never,* pay more for anything than that thing is worth to you at the time that you buy it. That way, you will never have occasion for second thoughts, and your enjoyment will be unencumbered by such considerations as the landlord knocking on the door demanding the rent. If you were to let things go that far, it's just possible that the Lone Ranger might not be able to rescue you.

In collecting for the future, Green Hornet Playing Cards can be a good deal.

Index